IN AND OUT OF ARKANSAS

Donna Mott

ISBN978-1-937862-53-4

Library of Congress Control Number 2013918786

Published by BookCrafters, Parker, Colorado.
SAN-859-6352, BookCrafters@comcast.net

Copies of this book may be ordered from
www.bookcrafters.net
and other online bookstores.

*Dedicated to
my children*

*Linda A. Mott, Terisa C. Mott,
Kathy A. Stocker, and B. Brian Mott*

Acknowledgements

I would like to thank my writers group,
The Writers Group of Clinton, Missouri,
for allowing me to read my stories aloud and for their
constant support in this endeavor.

I would also like to thank my proofreader and editor,
LA Mott.

Moving To Arkansas 1971-1972
Kansas City, Kansas

There was a lot going on between the year The Man and The Woman moved from a small town in Missouri to Kansas City and the year of the big move to Arkansas. The couple had four children who were progressing through school. The oldest girl was a freshman, the second girl was in the seventh grade, the third girl was in the second grade, and the boy was in kindergarten. The Man worked for a truck line picking up and delivering freight inner city. He belonged to The Teamster's Union and attended every meeting. The Woman worked at a distribution center packing and shipping jeans, overalls, and uniforms. She felt she could go to work since the youngest was now going to be in kindergarten.

It was a constant struggle to keep clean clothes for everyone and meals on the table. The two older girls were capable girls who could be relied on to help. The

Man was at home in the morning to see that the boy got to school.

The oldest had gradually become more involved with school activities, the other two girls made friends with some of the neighbors. The boy was almost never to be found as he was with a group of boys who played in a wooded area near the house. The youngest girl got herself ready every Sunday and hopped on any church bus that came by the house because they served Kool-Aid and cookies at Sunday school.

Getting the youngest, Brian, ready for Kindergarten was a chore. She corralled him late in the summer to begin scrubbing the imbedded grime from his hands as he and the boys were digging caves and making forts from dawn to dusk. While The Man was cutting his hair, The Woman told him he had better supervise a bath. The boy needed a good scrubbing while they had him in their clutches.

The first day of school the boy came home to report that he had been forced to put his head down on his desk for a nap, "And damn! That hurt my nose," he complained. The woman was relieved that the boy hadn't escaped from the school yard and couldn't believe someone had suggested he take a nap. He hadn't had a nap since he was one year old.

The Man had met a fellow who owned a race car. He helped Bill work on the car and The Man began going on out-of-town trips to various race tracks. Unknown to The Woman he drove the car in some of the races.

He also began spending a lot of time at a private club near the house. Sometimes The Woman would go with him when they were having something special going on. There seemed to be quite a few state officials there when they were having a party. The warden of a state prison, representatives, and such were there for special occasions. Once she met Satchel Paige and his wife who was catering a fund raiser for The Democratic Party.

Someone had given The Man tickets to the governor's birthday party in Topeka. The Woman spent all afternoon at the beauty parlor and dressed as well as she could. The party was a fund raiser which was a dinner of tough steak and speeches. The Woman was surprised when they also received invitations to the governor's inauguration. Of course, The Man and The Woman were not financially able to attend such a grand affair. The Woman didn't enjoy these events anyway, as no one seemed to be having a good time. She usually was sitting at a table with five or six drinks in front of her while The Man was tending bar and talking to everyone. She decided she would rather be with her children than these people, so she seldom went with him. She did go to the party they had for a guy who was going to jail for running an illegal gambling operation. This was such a funky idea she couldn't pass it up. However, she instructed her daughter to come to the club at nine o'clock and tell the person behind the bar to inform her that she was there to pick her up.

"Your father said that he would only have to tend

bar for an hour, but I know how that goes, and I am not going to sit up there all night."

She was seated with two couples and two men who were with a woman at a large table The Woman didn't know any of them. One of the men was the owner of a large truck line. Even though his wife was by his side, he began to make remarks to The Woman. It was evident he had already had plenty to drink. The Woman was uncomfortable with the way he was talking to her. She would never go tell The Man, in fact, she was worried he might overhear some of the remarks. The Man would cause quite a ruckus over the situation. But she knew that Linda would be there soon and sure enough a girl from upstairs came to tell her that her daughter was there. The Woman got up and walked out. Later she found out the owner of the club barred the man who had been sitting with her from ever coming back.

This was the last time she went to this club. Later, The Man had asked her if she wanted to go out two or three times. She thought this was great until she realized that they were going to clubs in North Kansas City and he didn't seem to know anyone there. They would bar hop for a couple of hours and then go home. She didn't know what that was about, but it was no fun and she stopped going with him at all. He was only at home for short periods of time and was in a grouchy mood when he was there.

The Woman spent any spare time she had reading books and painting. Beth, the wife of one of his friends, and The Woman decided to go out since their husbands had gone hunting over the weekend. There was no place to go except the movies. They stopped at a bar and grill. The Woman, even though she was older than Beth, could not be served without a birth certificate. The Woman thought it was ridiculous anyway since she didn't really like sitting in a bar. Another time they decided to go to a seminar that was being held in a church building. There was to be a speaker and discussion on the subject of psychic, telepathic, clairvoyant powers. The room was set up with a lectern and chairs. To the left as they walked in were pitchers of ice water and glasses, napkins and a coffee urn with Styrofoam cups. The other people attending were not unusual; in other words they didn't look like a bunch of wild eyed kooks. The Woman and Beth sat down on the second row.

The speaker began by saying that there would be a break when everyone could get acquainted and have some coffee or water. As he got on into his talk, The Woman was intent on what he was saying when Beth whispered in her ear, "There are two guys eyeing us. When break time comes, walk to the back like you are going to get something and then go out and run like hell."

The Woman nodded without looking up. When break time came the two women walked casually to the back, Beth pushed open the door and they ran to the car. Beth got the car started and pulled out onto the street. When The Woman looked back she could see the two guys standing on the curb.

She turned to Beth and said, "Let's go someplace and get a cup of coffee."

Beth drove until she saw an all night breakfast restaurant. When they walked in, a salt shaker whizzed past in front of their eyes. They heard one of the cooks yell that he had called the police.

The Woman looked at Beth, "Hurry, we have to get out of the parking lot before the police get here!"

For the second time that night they ran to the car and thanks to Beth's excellent driving while under stress they got away before the police got there. The Woman and Beth gave up trying to go out.

One day The Woman was washing her hair when she heard a knock on the door. There was a policeman. He asked about her son, who happened to be at home. The son was seven years old. The policeman said that some boys accused him of stealing a bike. After talking awhile the policeman said maybe her son should find some new playmates. The Woman thought about this a lot.

In 1968 Martin Luther King was killed. The Woman worked with several African-American women. She continued to go to work even though the riots had started. The women she worked with were very concerned about their safety. The Woman and The Man had an arrangement so he would pick her up at noon and she would take the car home after work. Then she would go pick him up when he got off work at nine that night. During the riots, the only people on the streets were the National Guard. The week of Good Friday the children were out of school so The Man decided to take the children to Union Station and put them on the train to Warrensburg to spend the weekend with their grandparents. He thought they should experience a train ride before the trains stop running. The kids were delighted to be going on the train by themselves. The Man and The Woman would go get them Saturday afternoon.

That evening, The Man made his usual preparations to go out. He stood in the doorway for a few seconds, "Joe needs me to help out tonight." He was gone then.

The Woman had thought maybe they would go someplace together since the kids were gone. But as she watched him, she realized he had his own agenda and it didn't include her. If she hadn't known before, it was clear now that he was no longer with the family. She sat down with a cup of coffee and a cigarette. She began to doodle on a piece of paper. She drew a line down the center. She listed her name and those of the kids on one side and The Man's name on the other. She sat as she did so often, drinking coffee and smoking one cigarette after another.

She had become very angry with him, she had thrown her rings at him, she had told him she hated him, and he left for awhile. The separating didn't work simply because they couldn't afford it. So, there it was, they couldn't afford to get a divorce. She had a dream that night that she was walking up stairs that were alabaster white. She was walking into a rainbow. She stopped to look back and there was The Man. He was in the dark with his hand on the newel post watching her. She seemed to take this for a sign that they should stay together. She quit expecting anything from him other than paying the rent and taking care of the cars. She stopped wasting her time and energy thinking he would ever change.

The Man hurt his back at work while loading a refrigerator on a truck. He was off work until the doctor released him to go back. He was compensated a substantial sum. While working on the race car, he and his friend talked about pooling their money and trying to find some property in Arkansas. They thought the two of them could build chicken houses like they saw in that part of the country. The dream was to have some property they could retire to. They drove to Arkansas one weekend to see what they could find. They had no luck until they stopped to visit The Man's uncle. He told them the Bean's place up on the side of the hill from his farm was for sale. The property consisted of eighty acres and there was a house on the place. So they started the process of buying the rocky brushy land.

The Woman was beginning to have pain in her arms every afternoon at work. The doctor said it was arthritis. This was getting worse especially when the fumes were bad in the warehouse. She figured she was going to have to quit her job. It was shortly after this that they signed the papers to buy the Arkansas land. The two couples drove down together to sign papers and the wives got to see the place.

Ellie, the other woman, was running a lunch counter in Kansas City, at the time. Bill was still working as a machinist. They agreed there should be someone living in the house so it wasn't sitting vacant. The Woman jumped at the opportunity to get the kids out of the city. If the men got some chicken houses started, maybe they could all live out here on this mountain.

The two couples loaded up their pickup trucks every Thursday with lumber, tools, furniture, food, and anything that would be of use to get the house and property fixed up. During the following year nearly every Friday after work they took one or two of the kids and drove to Arkansas. On the way they always stopped to eat fried chicken at The Blue Top Café at Lamar. They were always nearly starved by the time they got this far which was about halfway between Kansas City and that hill in Arkansas.

Ellie would bring lots of food from her café and over the weekend she would cook for everyone. Ellie was a short stout woman. She had snow white hair that was done up at the beauty shop every week. She drove a big Mercury sedan and had to have her coffee and cigarettes and Kansas City Star newspaper every where she went. She knew how to cook for a big group and invited The Man's Uncle Clyde, Aunt Georgia, and cousins, Pat and William. Sometimes cousins, Calvin and Louise and their son came up the hill to visit.

Every weekend was spent working cutting wood, clearing brush, and tearing down two old sheds. The men had to learn how to sharpen chain saws and try to avoid hitting rocks while sawing. They talked to Clyde to learn more about how to do things and who to see about building ponds. Clyde was a character. He had a mean streak like many from East Texas but was very charming. Now he had a new audience who would appreciate the stories that he had picked up and reworked over the years. He was involved in Arkansas politics. Clyde raised chickens and turkeys. Most of his time was taken up by keeping watch over his poultry houses. He had worked in the oil fields and had worked on his place for many years. He and his son William had both been injured in the oilfields. William was in a wheelchair; Clyde had been nearly blinded in one eye from poison gas at an oil rig. Also, Georgia had lost an arm as a child at a saw mill. Pat had polio as a child and walked with a limp. All these people were able to do as much or more than those who had no disabilities.

First Days in Arkansas
1972

Finally, in the spring of 1972 The Woman was able quit her job and move to Arkansas. As soon as school was out for summer vacation, they moved into the little house. The oldest daughter, Linda, graduated from high school and she stayed in Kansas City to attend college. The second daughter, Terisa, was already out of school for the year and she was staying with Uncle Clyde and Aunt Georgia in order to help him with his chicken houses. Terisa and Clyde got along very well in spite of his reputation of being a rather tough and obstinate man.

They bought an old truck and since The Man would still be working and staying in Kansas City, they would only have his paycheck to live on.

Ellie continued to cook up big meals for everyone on Saturday evenings. It was a fun time listening to Clyde's stories. Bill and The Man were gradually learning what was involved in a chicken and cattle operation. They asked him why this place was called Brother Adam's Mountain.

"Well, I don't know who told you that. Whoever told you that was probably just pulling your leg. Some of these old guys will tell you anything."

*****

The Man and Bill and Ellie were all on their way back to Kansas City. It was Sunday and The Woman was washing the breakfast dishes. She looked around and realized there was no turning back now. She dried her hands and went out to the front porch. The Woman and her two youngest kids walked down the road to a clearing by the pond. As she walked The Woman looked at the scenery with a new sense of belonging. The sunshine was wonderful and she could see for miles across the misty blue hills. There was a good sized wild strawberry patch here and although the berries were small they picked enough to take back to the house.

*****

Eleven year old Kathy had been observing how Ellie worked in the kitchen and now began putting some of these ideas to work. Ellie always had an abundance of gallon pickle jars from her cafe which she used for iced tea and other things. Kathy made a gallon of tea and put it on a shelf in the back room. Then she baked a heart shaped chocolate cake and a yellow cake. Later Clyde came up to see if they were lonesome. Kathy and her nine-year-old brother, Brian, were acting so silly The Woman thought he might never come back. After he left Terisa began heating up the leftovers from yesterday for supper. The next morning The Woman woke up to hear Kathy and Brian laughing in the kitchen with Clyde. The Woman was struggling to get her eyes open when she realized Kathy was still in her 'Ellie mode' and had fixed sausage, eggs, toast, and orange juice for breakfast. Clyde told her he didn't believe he cared for any as he had already eaten. The Woman suspected he didn't trust what an eleven year old had whipped up.

After Clyde left they got ready to go to town. The old model truck that had been purchased for The Woman would not start. The Woman changed clothes and went to the garden to work. She was trying to show Kathy and Brian how to hoe the weeds. But soon she discovered that Brian was lying down between the rows of green beans and Kathy was shoveling dirt on him. Clyde came back to the house to pick up Terisa to help him at the chicken houses. When he found out the truck wouldn't start, he hooked a chain on the bumper and pulled it until it started. While they were messing with the truck Kathy made lemon bread and two gallons of tea. The Woman changed clothes again and started out the door to go to town. As she was leaving, Kathy dropped a gallon jar of tea on the cement floor in the back room.

Finally, The Woman was able to go on to Huntsville;

however when she stopped at the service station to get gas the truck wouldn't start. The service station owner started the truck for her at no charge and The Woman went home without getting any of her errands done in town.

Clyde came back that afternoon and told her to take the truck down to Calvin and see if he could fix it for her. The Woman wondered what Clyde must think about this hopeless woman being dumped in his neck of the woods.

While Calvin worked on the truck The Woman visited with his wife, Louise. Louise gave her a gallon jar of milk from their cow and some turnip greens out of her garden. Calvin fixed the truck so it would start and told her she had better pick up some brake fluid the next time she went to town.

Back at home the self-appointed cook was busily making taffy which was something The Woman wouldn't try on her best day. The Woman was forced to have a little talk with Kathy and let her know they were not running a pastry shop. As she was doing this she looked out the front window and espied Brian at the top of a spindly walnut tree. He was quite content there with the breeze blowing the tree to and fro. Below the tree the ground was a hard rocky surface. She was used to seeing him shinny up trees, but the branches on this tree seemed brittle. Besides he was heavier than he used to be. Remembering a story her father told her about a similar situation, she remained calm. She went to the door and told the boy that it was time to eat. When he came down, she did not strangle him, but told him he should find a sturdier tree to climb and not to climb that tree again.

The Woman then began to make chocolate milk with the milk that Louise gave her. She was afraid the kids wouldn't like raw milk. When Kathy got the milk out of the refrigerator, she dropped it. There was another broken jar and a big mess on the kitchen floor. Ellie would have to bring another supply of gallon pickle jars next week.

Brian went to dig some worms in case they would go fishing. There wasn't any type of worm that could live in that rocky soil. The Woman told him they would buy some if she ever got to town. Terisa asked, "When are we going home?"

*****

There were many things to keep the kids busy; they often went swimming in the King's River, they picked blackberries, or went into the woods and pushed over dead trees. On the weekends the people who visited brought kids with them and they went fishing or swimming. The Woman decided since the truck was a nearly worn out anyway she would teach them all how to drive a stick-shift vehicle. The field by the house was bigger than a football field so they drove in a circle, taking turns. Brian could barely reach the pedals and see out, but he and the girls learned quickly and The Woman didn't have to ride with them. Clyde made good use of the young kids teaching them how to help him with the chickens and later with turkeys. Clyde had supervised roustabouts in the oil fields and was a very tough guy, but he evidently had patience enough to teach the city kids how to help. So, The Woman supposed the kids were actually helping him or he would run them off. He helped her whenever he could when they ran into difficulty with the truck or the well pump.

*****

At the end of summer, it was time to enroll the kids in school. She got the boy into grade school and Kathy into middle school with no problem. But when she and Terisa went up the hill to the high school she encountered problems. The powers that be tried everything to keep Terisa out. First, they did not want to give her credit for art classes she had in Kansas City. They also told her there was no room left in any of the business courses. And, furthermore, they had a dress code at this school. The girls wore dresses and if it was cold, they could wear pants under their dresses. The boys must have short hair and no beards or facial hair. The Woman then took Terisa to Kingston as that school was in their district also. That school had the same rules, but no bus could pick her up. The Woman went back to the Huntsville school and after haggling with them, they worked out a plan. Since Terisa only needed one English class to

16

graduate, they would accept her art credits, and she would only attend the one class. After talking to Aunt Georgia she managed it so Terisa could do volunteer work at the library until it was time to catch the bus to come home. Then Terisa and The Woman drove to Fayetteville to buy her skirts and blouses. The Woman took Terisa to school the first day and there were girls in blue jeans and boys with long hair and beards just like the kids in Kansas City. The Woman figured that the fact that she was from Kansas City must have been what set them off in the first place.

*****

The Man occasionally had a three day weekend which could be unpleasant as he usually had some type of work planned. He walked in one Thursday while Kathy was making meatloaf.

"What are you doing in here?" He growled.

The Woman walked in from outside.

"Why in the hell do you let that kid slop around with that meat? Nobody wants to eat anything a kid has messed around with."

Kathy scooted off to the bathroom to wash her hands and swish went the curtain that closed off the girl's room. The Woman didn't even answer him. She finished the meatloaf and shoved it into the oven and got some pork chops out to cook for supper.

The Man pulled open the curtain, "You two little fat

girls get your gloves on; we're going to cut some firewood this evening before it gets dark." To The Woman he said, "Jason and Loretta may come down tomorrow."

Brian was already standing by the tractor because he knew he would be working when The Man was at home. The Woman remembered why she moved here.

*****

The Woman and the kids had just returned from the river where they had a good time floating on big inner tubes and swimming. They watched Max and Carl trying to shoot fish with bows and arrows. The insurance man had told her about the time he and Max and some other boys had set fire to Kings River when they were in high school. They poured twenty gallons of gasoline on the river and set fire to it. He said the fire flowed down the river as the water moved. So she was not surprised that they were shooting fish. When The Woman and kids got dressed after coming home, they went down to see Louise. Louise gave them milk every few days. Today she asked The Woman if she would like to have some chickens. The chicken catchers sometimes missed a few chickens when they picked them up during the night. When The Woman took them, she and Terisa exchanged ominous looks. The Woman knew she had no place to keep them and Louise expected that they would dress them and put them in the freezer. Kathy and Brian were naming them on the way home thinking they would be pets. But the chickens wouldn't last long loose in the yard. There were wild animals roaming around looking for food all the time. When they got to the house The Woman put a big pot of water on the stove and began looking for the little hatchet. Kathy began begging her not to kill the chickens. Brian found his hatchet that he had bought at a dime store and they went to look for a suitable place to kill the chickens. When the water was hot Terisa and The Woman carried the pot out to the field. First, The Woman held the chickens one at a time on a log while Brian whacked at the necks with the dull hatchet.

"Sorry Charlie," He would say each time he chopped on a chicken's neck.

Meanwhile from a window of the house came the loud screams that could be heard for miles.

"Murderers, murderers, murderers!"

Terisa and The Woman managed to get some of the feathers off one chicken. When they got it cut open Brian was pulling the entrails out.

"Hey, there are worms in here. And poop. What is poop doing inside these chickens?"

Well, that did it for The Woman. She knew the chickens wouldn't be fit to eat. She took them to the edge of the field and threw them into a ravine. "The varmints will have a feast tonight."

The murderers went to the house intending to take showers. To their dismay they found that Kathy had locked the doors. After much begging and cajoling she unlocked the doors and went to her room which was closed off with a curtain. She swished the curtain closed in such a way that if it had been a door it would have slammed in a more satisfactory manner. The Woman fixed a glass of wine for herself and root beer floats for the kids. Kathy didn't speak to them for two days. The Woman vowed never to attempt butchering chickens again. Louise could probably dress a chicken with her eyes closed.

*****

Kathy and Terisa were having an argument about whose week it was to wash dishes. This was nothing new. No one wanted to wash dishes. The girls thought Brian should have to. But there were many times he had to help The Man when they were inside. The Woman asked them if they wanted to take over Brian's job. They didn't. Now this argument was approaching a fever pitch. The Woman told Kathy it was her turn. Then she wanted to argue with The Woman. The Woman tired of that and began marking an x on each day after Kathy's week to wash dishes. Kathy asked her what she was doing. The Woman told her that each time she opened her mouth to continue this argument would be another day of dish washing added on. Swish went the curtain, the argument was over.

*****

Every time there was a problem with the well pump or the truck it would be when The Man was gone. Clyde or Calvin would help in an emergency as when the truck wouldn't start and the pump wasn't working the same day. They were out of water, out of food, and the TV was out of order. The boy was better at coping with some things than The Woman. When the truck key dropped down in the window of the truck, Brian got the screwdriver and took the panel off the door. After retrieving the key, he put the panel back on.

*****

The Arkansas Conservation Department offered 1000 pine trees at a minimal cost. The Woman ordered them. When they came Clyde showed her how to plant them. She strode off into the briars and the bushes where a rabbit wouldn't go with an iron bar that weighed twenty pounds to begin planting the trees. When she looked back to get her bearings, she saw that Black Dog was following behind pulling up the trees she had just planted. After she straightened him out, she continued on. She planted pine trees for three weeks. All she could do then was hope it rained enough to keep them alive.

*****

Clyde was in the kitchen teaching the kids how to roll cigarettes. When he smoked a 'roll your own' the burning tobacco was falling out of the paper onto his shirt. Georgia could roll them better and that was with only one hand. Frequently, The Man would bring cigars home that were given to him by new fathers. The Man had never smoked. Occasionally The Woman would smoke one but they usually stayed on the table until someone happened by who appreciated them. Brian began sitting back in the big recliner smoking cigars while watching TV. The Woman finally put a stop to the cigar smoking because the kid was enjoying it too much.

*****

Clyde told the kids there were Indians living up the road. Brian wanted to know if we could invite the Indians to eat with us at Thanksgiving. Clyde told him that they raised dogs to eat and probably didn't eat turkey. Later, The Woman had to tell Brian not to pay too much attention to what Clyde said. The two Indian ladies actually were retired teachers and had a small farm and garden. The Woman did not invite them over for Thanksgiving.

*****

Linda called. She has been learning to fly a plane, but now she is getting ready to parachute jump out of a plane. The Woman knew she was wasting her breath but warned her not to do this.

*****

Brian tried riding his bike in the pond. He also tried walking around in the pond with his clothes on. He enjoyed sitting in the wood box pretending to be an astronaut.

*****

Clyde brought the kids a baby raccoon. They kept it for a week.

*****

Brian found a pack rat's nest and is duty bound to report the comings and goings of the rat. The Woman put him to work emptying mouse traps. He received twenty-five cents for each one and fifty cents if the mouse was alive. This was on the condition that he not show the creatures to any of the women or girls in the house.

*****

The Woman helped Terisa take care of Clyde's chickens so he could go to Little Rock to the Democratic convention. He was a good friend of Governor Faubus. But since Orville Faubus had moved on, he was now campaigning for the new guy.

Where The Three Rivers Began
Arkansas

During the move to Arkansas after purchasing land and a house with their friends, Bill and Ellie, The Man kept them informed about points of interest in the area. One thing he talked about frequently was where the three rivers began. The Kings River, War Eagle River, and White River were said to have all started in the same place. At a spot in Red Star, when it rained, water would run off the roof of a one-room school house. As it ran off it divided into three streams. Here, there was just a trickle of water going in three directions. As the stream picked up going down the mountain, it turned into three rivers which were each quite wide rivers at times. One starting west, one going northeast and the other went northwest.

One day Ellie suggested they all go to Red Star to see where the three rivers began. The Woman smiled to herself. She had been on trips such as this with The Man before. What usually happened was that as they drove along he would point out something a half mile away on the side of a hill. They would whiz by so fast The Woman wouldn't see anything but trees. But, never the less, it would be an interesting ride.

They headed down Highway 127 to Highway 16 on the journey to Red Star. If you want to go to Red Star you'd better get an old map or ask an old timer from the area where it is. On second thought, better get a map rather than have a witty fellow in overalls make a sweeping gesture with his arm taking in half the state of Arkansas and telling you, "There ain't much over there at Red Star any more, but it used to be over on the other side of Buzzard Mountain." It seemed to The Woman there was a Buzzard Mountain everywhere you go in the Ozarks.

It was a beautiful drive on Highway 16. There was a variety of wild flowers and the trees were looking their best. The Man pulled off onto the shoulder of the highway. Sure enough, there was a stick about the size of a tomato stake. Nailed to it was another stick with the words "Red Star" printed on it. They got out of the car. There was enough space on the shoulder to walk around. On one side was a field of tall grass with brush and trees around the edge. Across the highway they could see a rusty gate and a lane winding up a hill. Beyond that, the group could see nothing but trees and wildflowers or weeds (depending on who you were talking with). The Woman heard The Man tell Bill that the old school house was probably up that lane if it was still standing. They got back in the car and made a circle around to Kingston where they bought some snacks and Pepsi Cola. It was a short drive from there back home. The Man and Bill left the house shortly after to go see his Uncle Clyde.

As soon as they left, Ellie looked at The Woman and asked, "Did we see where the three rivers start?"

The Woman laughed, "I don't know, maybe we blinked."

Trash, Septic Tanks, Wells and The Earth 1972 - Arkansas

"What do we do with the trash?" The Woman asked The Man. She was becoming educated about the fact that out here in the boonies there was no trash service, the well was filled by a spring, and waste water went into a septic tank. The owners of the property had to deal with these things.

The Woman realized that she would be polluting the air by burning trash. Furthermore, she would be taking cans, bottles, and things that wouldn't burn to a ravine on the property. This was disgusting to her, but there was no other solution. Once when The Man stopped to see a fellow about buying a flat bottom boat, The Woman stayed in the truck while they talked. She was appalled to see two young children playing outside among the piles of jars, bottles, and cans. These people didn't have a ravine so they threw the trash out the front door.

The septic tank was a mystery although it apparently was something that was working. She never understood where the water came from that was filling the cistern type well. It was a spring, but where did it come from? When there was a problem with the well, there was no water.

It was then she realized that humans were destroying the planet; they didn't seem to belong here.

Everything The Man and The Woman did was not good for the land. They had a helicopter come to spray several acres to kill the brush and second growth trees where someone before them had clear cut most of the land. The Woman was the one who had to go up in the helicopter to show the pilot where to spray. Everything looked so different from the air; she hoped she showed him the right places to spray. She was at home when he sprayed the trees. She wondered what effect that would have on her health. They were sowing fescue seed for grass that wild birds and animals couldn't eat.

The good things they did were to build ponds and stock them with fish. Eventually they began sowing other grasses and planting trees.

The Woman noticed something else after living on Brother Adam's Mountain. The view from this height made it obvious that the earth was always moving. As she watched the hills and sky, she could see that everything about her was changing constantly every minute, not day-by-day or in four seasons a year.

Hippies, Lesbians, and 'Back To The Land' Couples 1972 to 1980 - Arkansas

The Sixties Kids

The area around Brother Adam's Mountain was a magnet for the back-to-the-land movement.

The sixties kids, who the locals labeled hippies, flower children, and long-haired yahoos drove, walked or floated in. The locals looked upon them with disdain. There were some couples who were making an honest effort at building a real mini-farm. The Foxfire books and Mother Earth News was prevalent. Even The Woman had copies that her family had given her. She tried making elderberry wine and turnip kraut among other projects, but she was not into the serious business of raising chickens, composting and getting into the science of the year-around garden. At the big commune near Kingston the people there had built cabins and were actually trying to raise most of their food and other items they thought they needed. This seemed to be on a map, because they attracted people from as far away as California. In fact, some were children of movie stars and other celebrities. Different groups rented the stone house at the end of the road for a week or a month at a time. This house had no water or electricity; it was simply a shelter. The Woman would see them at times walking past her house and walking on those rocky hilly roads was not easy. Any time The Woman saw them walking to town, she gave them a ride and she let them use her telephone. While walking one day she came upon several young women that she had become acquainted. They were having a discussion about E.S.P. and other paranormal subjects. The Woman told them she had found that quite often she could guess a person's middle name if she had time to think about it. One of these women said her name was Mariah and could she guess her middle name?

After they had walked almost to The Woman's house, she said, "I don't think Mariah is your real name."

The Woman never saw this person again.

She stopped on her way home to visit some of the people who were camped in the stone house because The Woman wanted to see the fawn they had rescued. Most of the women were dressed in long skirts and shirts tied at the waist giving them a gypsy like appearance.

One of the women gave The Woman a moonflower seed. Given the manner in which this was offered, The Woman wondered what she was supposed to do with it.

"Is this for good luck or am I supposed to eat it or what?" The Woman asked.

"Plant it," the other woman said.

The Woman thought to herself, *Well, you never know unless you ask.*

Women would drift in and start building log cabins while living in tents, but they soon learned that they didn't have the 'know how' or equipment for such a venture. Even though The Woman was raised on a small farm, she realized that her mother and father had done the managing of it all and she knew very little about gardening, canning or raising animals. Most of these people knew less than she did.

There was a popular song at that time about a purple school bus filled with hippies who pulled into a little town and eventually became solid citizens there. One day The Woman and kids were returning from town. As she turned the pickup toward home, there by the stone house was a purple school bus. She nearly drove into the ditch when she spied the next sight.

"Take a good look kids, there's Jesus. He has returned!"

And there walking up the dusty road was a fellow with long white hair and long flowing white beard. He was dressed in sandals and white robe that was being blown about in the breeze.

The Woman slowed down some so as not to raise the

dust as she passed him. She wondered what she might see next. What she saw the next time she went to town was the purple bus broken down on the side of a steep hill. It stayed there until some of the local people called Sheriff Baker to come out and tell Jesus and his followers they would have to move the bus off the narrow road.

Most of these travelers moved on. Some had dreams of becoming artists or writers. Susan was the only person The Woman knew of who was really selling art. She was a brilliant woman and even though she enjoyed her life out on the hill, she went to the university to continue her studies. She eventually moved to Fayetteville to work at the university. She continued to raise chickens, garden, illustrate books, and write.

The Air Pistol
1972 – Arkansas

Bill Curtis had an air pistol complete with a belt and holster. He set up some targets on the old shed in back of the house. He told Terisa, Kathy, Brian and The Woman to come out there and he would teach them to shoot the pistol. They spent the afternoon taking turns shooting. The Woman didn't think she could hit the target, but it was either a pellet gun or a BB gun so the shot scattered. She soon could hit the target somewhat accurately. The kids were hitting the targets easily. Bill was a good teacher.

Bill handed the gun and holster to The Woman. "Why not wear this when you are out walking? There are probably snakes all around here." The Woman wasn't too sure of this, but she let him talk her into wearing the gun and holster. She felt like a gunslinger from the old west.

The Woman wore the gun whenever she was hiking through the woods, but she never saw a snake.

One day she and the kids were in the back room which had a cement floor. She had been outside and took the belt off that was holding the holster. The pistol slipped out and hit the floor. It went off and pellets hit the ceiling thankfully missing everyone in the room. The ceiling was covered with the type of tile that had little pinpoint holes in each tile. The Woman and the kids all had the same thought, *Hope he doesn't notice the new holes in the ceiling,* meaning The Man, because he noticed everything.

The Woman put the gun on the shelf intending to give it back to Bill when he and Ellie and The Man came on the weekend.

The weekend went by without anyone mentioning the holes in the ceiling. The Man left on Sunday to go to Kansas City. Bill and Ellie were leaving later. Before they left Bill asked, "Who shot up the ceiling?"

The Woman told him what had happened. She said, "I think you'd better take this gun. It went off when I dropped it and could have hit one of us. How did you see those little holes anyway?"

He said he saw it the minute he walked in because of the pattern of the holes.

Clyde's Big Hog
1973 - Arkansas

The days had been hot and dry. The Woman and the kids were carrying their fishing poles to a pond down by Clyde's chicken house. They could hear the big fans sucking the hot air out of the house to keep the chickens cool. Clyde drove his truck over to the side door. Soon he was throwing dead chickens into the back of his truck.

The Woman went over to talk to him. "What do you do with those chickens? Do you have to bury them?"

He didn't answer right away but when he brought out the last chicken he said, "Foller me when I start up. And bring the younguns, I want to show you something."

He took off down a rough logging road through the brush. The Woman and kids walked behind the truck that came to a stop in a clearing.

Clyde backed his truck to a stoutly built boarded pen. "Come over here kids." He threw a chicken into the pen. A huge five hundred pound hog ran over and ate the chicken, bones, feathers and all in about three minutes.

"Do you all see that?" Clyde looked at Brian. "Hey, boy, do you see that?" he asked as he threw two more chickens at the monster. "That hog will eat anything that gets in the pen so don't ever come down here by yourself."

They watched, mesmerized, as the hog ate all five chickens. They could hear it crunching the bones as it gobbled up the feast Clyde brought. Clyde emptied a five gallon bucket of water over the fence into a tub and he was ready to go.

Clyde went on to his house and the family walked back to the other road to the pond. The Woman didn't think she had to worry about any of the kids messing around that hog pen. She knew it was one of the scariest things she had ever seen.

Local Dialect and Parking in Huntsville 1972 - Arkansas

It took awhile to learn the dialect of this region. The Woman and her friend Ellie talked about this over coffee. They puzzled over several expressions they heard frequently. Sometimes they were forced to ask Clyde or Georgia to explain. They repeatedly heard people remarking that they were going to "Federal" to shop. Well, The Woman and Ellie wanted to go to Federal. But they couldn't find it on the map. They thought maybe it was in Oklahoma but didn't think it was in Missouri. Finally they asked Georgia. She explained, "Fayetteville was taken over by the union army during the civil war. People around here have called it Federal ever since."

*****

37

When The Woman went to Huntsville soon after moving, she went into the dime store.

A voice from behind the counter called out, "Are you all alright?"

The Woman was slightly surprised at this but replied that yes, she was alright. Then she went around the store to the counter that had combs and mirrors and looked to see if she was pale or otherwise seemed strange. She didn't see anything out of place. As she went on with her shopping, another customer came in.

The Woman heard this same voice call out, "Are you all alright?"

The customer answered, "Ahm alrait, are ye all alrait?"

"Oh yes, we're fine."

The Woman had learned another bit of this new language. She would have to go home and practice saying "Are ye all alrait?"

*****

She went from the store to the newspaper office to get a subscription to The Madison County Recorder. There was a woman outside sweeping the sidewalk. She stopped sweeping so she could talk to The Woman. She was interested to know about where she moved to. They talked about their children. She talked about her son. The Woman went in then and ordered her paper and the lady outside went on with her sweeping. The Woman was telling Georgia about this later.

Georgia said, "Oh, that was Altus Faubus. She owns the newspaper now. Her husband married a younger woman and doesn't live around here anymore."

The Woman was surprised that a former governor's wife would be sweeping the sidewalk.

*****

Ellie and The Woman had another run in with the local dialect at the feed store. They were going to buy some seeds for the garden. When they went in there was a farmer and his wife who were laughing with the woman behind the counter. The clerk told Ellie and The Woman that some woman traveling through from St. Louis had been in the store asking for hominy seeds. After they all laughed at that, Ellie began looking around the store. The clerk asked her if she could help her. The Woman said they wanted to buy some radish and lettuce seeds. She asked if they wanted to buy them by the book. The Woman was thinking she could just pick up some little envelopes with pictures on the front and she would choose what she wanted. She knew nothing about buying by the book. She and Ellie looked at each other but said nothing. They bought some onion sets from a barrel. They hurried out of the store. Now they had another puzzle. Ellie had never planted a garden and The Woman had never heard of buying seeds by the book.

Back they went to Georgia who explained this one. The woman was saying, "Do you want to buy seed by the bulk?" In other words, not in little envelopes, but measured out by weight dipped out of cartons.

*****

The Woman managed to create quite a stir in Huntsville while parking in front of the laundromat. When she finished doing the laundry, she and the kids stood looking at the truck. There was a cement post about forty-five inches high in front of the parking space. But what they were looking at was that the post was between the bumper of the truck and the front of the truck. This meant the truck could not be moved forward or backward. The Woman stared at the truck wondering how she ever got the truck parked in such a way. She went to the grocery store which was next to the Laundromat, and the grocer after looking at the situation told her he would call a tow truck. By now there were a few interested men leaning against a wall waiting to see what was going to take place. But when the tow truck arrived there was quite a crowd gathering thinking there might have been a wreck. It was very amusing to them when they saw how this woman had wrapped her truck around a cement post. So they stayed to see if Ralph's wrecking service would be able to solve this problem. Ralph had the truck lifted off the post in a jiffy and charged The Woman five dollars. No doubt he was enjoying this as much as everyone else. The Woman had been in worse situations than this so she was past being embarrassed. The kids, of course, were as amused as the rest of the crowd in the parking lot.

Kingston, Arkansas
1972-1979

Kingston is a wide spot in the road on Highway 21 about five miles from the house on Brother Adam's Mountain. The Woman took the kids to explore the town and see if they could buy worms there.

There were stores in a semi-circle around a little plot of grass with a sign that said Kingston. These stores and the post office were at least a hundred years old. One store had clothes that The Woman recognized as being from the fifties. She wondered if the overalls would crack at the places where they had been folded. There were items that would be a collectors dream. There were snacks and a few grocery items. She told the kids she was going to move the truck over to the other side of the highway and look in the other stores so they could walk over there. When she looked back as she was moving the truck, there was Brian running along behind barking like a dog.

These crazy kids, The Woman thought, *They moo at the cows and now the people in the stores will think he is simple-minded.*

They walked toward the next store. As they approached the store they saw an old man sitting on a bench in front. He looked to be about ninety-five years old. A woman who was not quite that old came out and slammed the screen door, "Wake up, Dad, wake up, Dad!" She shook him until she was sure he was still alive and went back inside. The Woman and kids went in and talked to the two ladies there, but there was not much merchandise in the store. They walked past buildings that were ready to fall in. Clyde had told them there used to be a drug store here. He said they were always chasing the pigs out when it was in operation years ago. On the corner was a more modern grocery complete with refrigerated items and fresh bread. The Woman bought some things here and Terisa put them in the truck. They went on down to Pratt's store which was like a museum. The cash register and wood stove, rocking chair, glass top cases were all as they were at the turn of the century. They had a few grocery items here for sale. Mr. Pratt was an acquaintance of Clyde's. Clyde told The Woman to ask him to show her his antique coffins that were upstairs. The Woman didn't trust Clyde; it would be just like him to put his friend on the spot and cause The Woman to be in an embarrassing situation. The Woman knew that some places in this area still sold moonshine. She had suspected this might be one of the places. The Man had bought some already to show off to his friends but she didn't know where he got it. This was an interesting store and the town was gradually becoming a tourist attraction.

Later the town got a new post office which was built across the road from the old one. When it was finished the builders took the old loafer's bench over and placed it in front, just like the old post office. A reporter from the county newspaper asked one of the old timers how he liked the new post office. He thought for a moment and replied, "Well, it's ok I guess, but I never cared much for this part of town."

Campaigning President of Local 498 1973 – Kansas City and Huntsville

The Man had arrived at the home on Brother Adam's Mountain the night before from Kansas City, where he worked as an inner city truck driver. The whole family had eaten breakfast, and the kids were trying to become invisible as he usually had work lined up for the weekend.

But this morning he did not seem to be in a hurry to begin cutting wood or using the brush hog. Instead, he was cleaning and oiling his shotgun and rifle. He did this regularly.

The Woman was at the sink preparing a roast to put in the oven; Terisa could cook the rest of the meal. It was Kathy's turn to wash dishes.

After The Man put his guns away he came to the kitchen. He stood in the doorway with one hand against the door frame looking out the front window. Even though The Woman was facing away from him she could feel that he was still there.

"The boys want me to run for president of the local. They are tired of those two guys that are in there. Those two have been stealing from the local for years. The secretary and some others say they will help me. So I guess that is what I am going to do."

The Woman thought about this for a minute. When she turned around he had already gone out. She figured that was the end of the plans for chicken houses and a cattle operation which did not make her unhappy.

She heard the tractor running. The kids were getting a temporary break from picking up rocks and cutting wood.

The Man hugged and kissed everybody on Sunday as he was getting ready to go back to the city. "I probably won't come home next weekend. I have to get signs made up and bills printed to hand out. I am going to meet the men when they are getting off work. Our local represents men in Kansas, Missouri, and Arkansas. I will be traveling around to see as many people as I can over the weekend." Then he was gone.

Two weeks later The Man returned. He worked on The Woman's truck and cut firewood for the winter. The Woman and the kids helped pile brush and stack wood. The Man was excited about his campaign. The union members were ready for a change. Again he told them he wouldn't be back for two weeks.

Meanwhile The Woman had been canning green beans, making jelly, and putting food in the freezer. She had signed the boy up for Little League baseball. She took the kids swimming. Every now and then they would have company. Her brother brought their mother and father to visit. Her father fell in the pond while fishing. Her mother baked bread and made vegetable soup. The kids were delighted to see them.

When The Man came back he was agitated about how the campaign was progressing. "I have to ride around with a shotgun on my lap all the time. Those god-damned Mexicans are following me everywhere I go," he told her, as he went out the door on his way to find Bill.

After he went out, The Woman tried to make sense of what he just said. She knew that running for president of a Teamster local could be risky business, but Mexicans? How did Mexico figure in all this? He threw fragments of information out in such a way that The Woman could never grasp fully what he was dealing with. However, she thought, he could forget all that and live on Brother Adam's Mountain if he wanted to.

A few weeks later he was in a better frame of mind. He told The Woman that he had called Alex. Alex told Jerome to pull those Mexicans off. The Man continued on with his campaign.

Jerome? The Woman thought, *Jerome was supposed to be one of The Man's friends.*

The Man concentrated on getting a new wood stove

put in the house since the chimney had caught on fire at the end of last winter. He began cutting more firewood. He bought a different truck for The Woman, which was not much better than the other one.

The first of December The Woman went to Kansas City with The Man for the election. They went to see the oldest daughter. She had dropped out of college and became one of the first women to be hired by Southwestern Bell Telephone Company in Kansas City, Kansas as a residential installer, which was traditionally a man's job.

The Man took The Woman to a restaurant and then to a private club for a drink. Then they went to the union hall where friends of his had parked a big R.V. for them to sit in while the voting was taking place. They were not allowed inside the hall during the voting process. There were buses bringing in some of the voters. The opposition had paid for the buses, but the men were "voting for us" as some of the men were chanting. The voting was slow and lasted into the wee hours of the morning. The Woman had felt that she should dress for the party that usually took place after the votes were counted. She was becoming more uncomfortable by the hour in the confines of the R.V. When the votes were counted, The Man had won. But it was too late for a party. So instead, the winner and his wife went to his tiny rented room. There was only enough space for the bed and a night stand. He checked out the bathroom down the hall before The Woman used it because there were mostly traveling men staying there. They left early in the morning to go to Arkansas.

In January The Man took office. Shortly after there was a Teamster convention in Las Vegas; The Man told The Woman they would be going. This news struck fear into The Woman's heart. She had no desire to go to Las Vegas unless she would really be with The Man, but she knew that the wives got shuffled off to be entertained while the men were in meetings. She also worried about what kind of clothes she would need for this kind of an event. She stewed about this for a week. Then she was saved; The Man called and said the previous officers of the local had left the local broke. There was no money for The Man to go to the Teamster convention. Later there were other national conventions, but it was several years before The Woman was asked to go again.

Black Dog
1976 - Huntsville, Arkansas

During the summer after moving to Brother Adam's Mountain, the sixteen-year-old daughter began talking about getting a dog. She spoke to the cousins who lived down the road about it. And soon Pat and William told her they knew of a black lab and Irish setter mix that needed a home. The dog was very black except for a tiny bit of white on his lower lip. The Woman called the black Irish Setter/Labrador Retriever, "Black Dog," because of the humor of it. She wanted to name him Cat but the kids objected. Everyone but The Woman called him Blackie. He was so intensely black that was just the only name he could have. The kids liked Blackie; he was the only pet they had ever had other than their Dad's hunting dogs.

The Woman liked having Blackie accompany her on her walks through the woods. She never thought of him as being a guard dog until on one of their walks they happened to see some men working on the electric lines that went through the property. She heard The Black Dog growl deep in his throat. The Woman turned and walked the other way to avoid a problem with the dog

The dog seemed to know whether she was going for a walk or if she was going to town. If she was going shopping he didn't bother himself to get up from his place under the trees. Sometimes if she slipped out the front door to go walking he would run to catch up and whip her with his tail.

Black Dog didn't seem to be very aware of other animals. Once, they walked very near a little black bear and neither of them saw it until it ran to a brush pile. He did growl at The Man once when he and The Woman were having an argument. The Woman stopped arguing and went in the house for the dog's protection. Another time when the cougar with cub came within five hundred yards of the house, The Woman saw the Black Dog didn't have a clue it was anywhere near.

The Woman had the opinion for many years that dogs do think, contrary to some articles she had read. It was proved once again to her when The Man brought home a young Brittany Spaniel to train for pheasant and quail hunting. Whenever The Man was gone on a business trip, The Woman let the Brittany go walk with her and Black Dog. The young pup began to jump up on the bigger dog as they strolled along. The Brittany was grabbing onto Black Dog's ears. The Woman thought this was irritating so she picked up a long twig and swatted the pup with it hoping to teach it not to chew on the other dog's ears. After walking a little further, Black Dog stopped and fell behind. Then The Woman felt something tugging at the twig she had picked up. The black dog had gently taken the twig and laid it aside. The Woman was reminded once again that she was not in charge of anything.

When the weekly paper came out The Woman learned that the veterinarian in Huntsville drove around the county vaccinating dogs and cats. Listed in the paper were the stores and little towns where he would be and the date and time of day. The Woman could either take Black Dog to Kingston or to Bollingers' store.

On Wednesday at nine o'clock she let Black Dog in the cab of the truck. He had never ridden in the bed of the truck and she was afraid he would jump out. She tried to get the dog to stay on the floor but he had to sit on the seat to see out.

When she drove up to the store she left Black Dog in the truck and went inside. There she stood around with a group of men who were wearing overalls and faded blue shirts to wait for the vet. They talked about the weather and someone who had died last week. They were laughing about old Wes Brown who had bought some goats. He hoped the goats would eat the brush off the twenty acres he just bought.

The vet drove up then. He got his equipment arranged and asked who was first. The men were polite country men and allowed The Woman to get her dog's shots first.

The Black Dog behaved better than some of her kids when she took them to a doctor. The vet asked what the dog's name was and who the father and mother was. The Woman thought, *I always get asked questions I don't know the answers to.* She told him the dog's name was Black Dog and she didn't know the parents. He gave the dog the shots and checked him over. He told her the dog was too fat. Well, she knew that; Brian had told her fifty times in the last month that the dog was too fat. She didn't know why he was fat as he was an outdoor dog and she didn't feed him an excessive amount of food. Possibly he was eating someplace else. And she wondered how Brian noticed he was too fat.

At any rate, she got the dog his rabies shot without having to go to town with the dog. That was a good thing.

The Woman liked to go out on the front porch when it was dark and look at the lights that were sprinkled throughout the hills. It was hard to believe there were that many houses in the area. She could also see the lights from Eureka Springs on a clear night. The stars and moon lit up the landscape at times. As she stood stargazing in this manner one night, she turned to see the scariest sight she had ever seen: an ugly human-like face, which was only two feet high, was looking at her. She tried to scream but she was not a screamer and the only noise out of her mouth was "uh uh uh." She was three steps from the front door not that it would matter as this must be a creature from outer space. When she moved the black dog began to wag his tail. When she told Susan and Suzanne about her frightening experience, they said the black dog had come to their house and looked in the window. They were terrified until they realized what it was. The dog was so black that in the dark his face looked flat like a human face. When Ellie left one morning while it was still dark to go visit Bill in the hospital, the phantom dog nearly scared the daylights out of her too.

Snow and Fire
Arkansas

"We don't usually have much snow in this part of the country. Our winters are normally pretty mild."

Maybe they said "wild."

The Woman learned to listen to the weather forecasts. If they mentioned snow she had better go to town to stock up on groceries, jugs of water, and books from the library. There would be no school, the water pipes would probably freeze, it might be several days before the snow would melt off the roads. No one was going to plow the roads unless The Man was at home. Later, when Bill and Ellie moved to their place, he could get to town in his four wheel drive truck. The Woman could get out in an emergency.

At least once each winter she had to crawl around under the house in an effort to thaw out water pipes. Bill and The Man had rigged up a propane heater at the well-house to keep the pump from freezing. The well-house was the size of a small shed and the propane tank was outside. It was connected to the little stove inside with a pilot light that kept the shed warm.

Bill was in Kansas City and since they shared the well, he became concerned that the heater wasn't turned high enough to prevent the pump from freezing. He called The Woman to ask her if she would go out and turn the heater up a little more. She went to the well house and stepped inside. She had to push the door nearly closed in order to get to the heater as it opened into the shed. When she turned the heater up, the gas line which was attached to the stove with a nipple without a clamp, slipped off and flames went up the wall. The walls had been papered with tar paper and immediately caught on fire. The Woman pulled the door so she could get out. She went to the house to watch the well house burn to the ground. She thought about a poem she had copied and sent to her sister just last week. There was a line in the poem about fire coming up out of a hole in the ground. The Woman shivered. No water for sure now.

The next few weeks were spent figuring out how to exist without water. Gallons of drinking water were brought from town or from neighbors. Water from the pond was used to flush and heated for some bathing. As soon as The Man and Bill could get the new pump and materials to rebuild, they got to work and had water running once again.

Terisa Graduates
1973 – Arkansas

Terisa needed one English credit in order to graduate. Even though this was the only class she had to attend, she did not feel comfortable going for the one hour. She knew how many days she could miss and still get credit for the class and she missed them all. She did not have to study as the courses in Kansas City were ahead of this class.

She had one girl friend, but other than that she spent more time with the older women at the library and the county health department, where she volunteered. She was happy when Pat and William found the black dog for her. She and the other kids had always wanted a dog.

It was odd that she and Clyde got along so well. But, she was a good worker and he appreciated that. She was a curious mixture of shyness and 'I'm not taking anything off of anybody.' She didn't like the way The Man spoke to her and she was determined not to let anyone else speak to her in that tone of voice.

In Kansas City, The Woman was astounded to hear that Terisa had socked an African-American boy twice her size hard enough to nearly knock him off his feet. Luckily that situation got sorted out without too much trouble. But up until that time she had thought of Terisa as being extremely timid.

At the end of the school year she was supposed to have her senior picture taken. The Woman knew Terisa didn't really want to, but she talked her into it. Even then, Terisa tried to back out. Luckily the other girls in the class encouraged her to have her picture taken. It was a beautiful picture. Terisa refused to go to her graduation ceremony. She had her mind made up to leave as soon as school was out.

Terisa's grandmother sent money for her to take the bus to Warrensburg. Terisa hoped to get a job there and help her grandmother. In order to get on the bus she would have to go to Fayetteville which was forty miles away. The Woman's truck was in very bad shape. She wasn't even driving it to town any more. Shawandosa, one of the Indian women, drove to town every day. Terisa said two of the county health nurses were going to Fayetteville soon. So, The Woman drove Terisa to the road where Shawandosa picked her up. The two county nurses took her to the bus stop. The terrified Terisa had to change buses in Kansas City in order to get to Warrrensburg. This is how Terisa left home and left Arkansas.

Absentee Ballots Challenged
1974 - Arkansas

The Man and The Woman registered to vote soon after moving to Arkansas. Uncle Clyde and all the family including The Man and The Woman were voting straight Democratic ticket. Bill and Ellie and The Man voted absentee ballots. When the time came to vote The Woman drove down the hill to an old school house to cast her ballot. That was that, until the absentee ballots were challenged.

Soon there was a knock on her door. It was an F.B.I. agent who was documenting all the people in the county who voted absentee. He soon put The Woman at ease. He noticed a set of Hardy Boys Mystery books in the book case. He said he had read all these when he was a boy. She told them they belonged to her daughter in Kansas City. After chatting for a few minutes he left, satisfied that this house looked lived in. The notice, that she and The Man would have to appear in court with many other people to be questioned about absentee ballots, came in the mail. This made The Woman very nervous even though there was nothing wrong with her husband's ballot. Lawyers could be tricky, they might get her confused and she would say something wrong.

They had gone to court once to declare bankruptcy. That time she only had to stand behind her husband, who was seated in the witness chair. Every time he answered a question she was asked if that was true. So all she had to do was say, "yes" when she was asked. The Woman had gone into this experience not knowing what it would entail. Years ago, The Man had bought and sold guns, which was more of a hobby than a business. When he was asked about the guns he had, he said the guns had burned up in the fire. The Woman was sure her eye brows shot up and it was all she could do to keep from saying, "What fire?" But she said, "Yes, that's right." as calmly as possible. So now she was hoping The Man would be called up on the witness stand on this election thing before she was then she could follow what he said.

The week of the court appearance The Woman dug around in the closet to find a dress to wear. She realized she would have to go to town and get some panty hose. Since she wore Red Wing work boots most of the time she had no idea where her heels were. The Man was driving down from Kansas City and she hoped he would get to the court house before her. That morning when she dressed in her pink outfit she noticed the skirt was kind of short and the hose she bought were not panty hose which sent her into a fevered fit. When she and the kids left that morning she forgot her sweater, put her cigarettes in her daughter's purse which the girl then took to school, she ran over a turkey on the way to town. In the back of her mind was the thought that one of the sows was going to have babies that day.

The Woman arrived in court and sat down. She looked around to see if The Man was there. Of course, he was not there yet. In a short time her name was called. She walked through the gate and swore to tell the truth. She took a seat in this Federal Court room. The Republican lawyer asked her to state her name and address. She had no trouble with this.

Republican lawyer: "How long have you lived at this address?"

The Woman: "About two years."

Republican lawyer: "Who did you vote for?"

The Woman: "I voted straight Democratic ticket."

Democratic lawyer: "Objection, she did not vote absentee and is not required to answer."

The Republican lawyer asks something else The Woman didn't understand and luckily the Democratic Lawyer objected.

Republican lawyer: "Did you pick up a ballot for your husband?"

The Woman: "Yes I did."

Republican: "Is this your husband's signature on this request for an absentee ballot?"

The Woman is nervous now although she is sure it is The Man's signature, "I am not sure but I think he signed it."

The Republican lawyer asked if The Woman took some papers with her when she picked up the ballot. She said she didn't.

Then the Republican lawyer asked again in a different way if she had picked up a ballot for her husband.

The Woman was tiring of this and was not sure what he was saying, "I may be stupid, but I don't understand what you are talking about."

The judge said, "That's alright, we are not sure what he means either."

The Democratic lawyer had no questions and The Woman was free to go. The Man had arrived and it didn't take long for him to verify his signature on the request for a ballot.

The Man and The Woman went home in separate vehicles. As soon as she could change into her jeans and boots, they went out to see if there were any new little pigs. There were no little pigs to be seen.

The Man went back to Kansas City. The Woman was relieved that this ordeal was over. Soon the kids would be home from school and things would be back to what had become normal.

Surprise Visitors Visiting the Old Home Place - Yintz Family June

On a warm balmy day in June a pick-up truck and two cars drove up and parked in front of the little house on Brother Adam's mountain. The Woman and the three children peered out the windows wondering who was coming to visit today. Ever since they moved here it seemed that people had been coming from everywhere to visit.

The car doors opened and thirteen men and women who seemed to be sixty years of age and older piled out and began walking around the property. Some of the men were dressed in overalls and some were wearing slacks and sport shirts. Several women had dressed up in flower spattered cotton dresses. They placed some baskets and other belongings on the rock ledge in front that The Man and the boy built. There was no shortage of big boulders that The Man could move around with his tractor. He had even found three four foot long flat rocks to use for steps to the front porch. The Woman watched as the men pointed out the work that had been done with the rocks. They walked over to look at the new pond. Then they headed around to the back yard.

The Woman saw that these people were prepared to stay as they spread their lunch out on the rock ledge, so she went out to see what was happening.

"Hello, we were just wondering what you folks are doing here. Are you lost?"

A large woman wearing a summery dress walked over to her, "We are members of the Yintz family. We came by to visit the old home place. There used to be a cabin back behind this house. Some of us remember when grandma and grandpa lived there. The Yintzes owned all this land around here. We owned that big log house down the road there," she said as she pointed to Susan's house. "We didn't know the Beans had moved from here. We come back every year to visit the old home place and have a picnic."

The Woman went back inside to tell the kids who the invaders were. They found it very amusing that they had this to look forward to every year and that the Yintzes still felt they had some claim of ownership.

When she told Susan and Suzanne about this they said the same visitors came to their place every year. Susan showed The Woman the walls of the second floor of her house where the old logs were still visible.

Ouija Board
Arkansas

Ellie's daughter, Sandy and two granddaughters came to visit Bill and Ellie in their new mobile home which was a short distance from The Woman's house. Ellie had already taken them to Silver Dollar City and other than swimming there wasn't a lot to do. Ellie at some time earlier had searched until she found an Ouija Board. She and The Woman and her two girls had occupied their time playing with that on long afternoons. Ellie dug this out of her closet to help entertain Sandy and the kids. They brought it down to The Woman's house. Sandy and The Woman began turning the lights out and lighting candles. Sandy knew some tricks to make it seem like the spirits were coming around. They all decided it would be more fun if they went out to the root cellar and lit candles to see if the spirits would visit the Ouija board out there. Kathy had cleaned the musty old cellar out after they had tornado warnings. The Woman had forced them to go into the spider infested cellar and they were not going in there again until the spider webs, leaves, and acorns were swept out.

Brian and Ellie stayed in the house. They wanted to watch M*A*S*H* on television. Sandy and Kathy put a big cardboard box in the cellar and covered it with a cloth. They set up some folding chairs and an old lawn chair. As the sun was setting and the shadows were cast over the cellar they set several candles on the old oak shelves which years ago held rows of canned vegetables and jellies. The women who had put them there would frown upon such activities that were taking place here now.

As soon as everyone was seated and Sandy had her two girls, Patsy, and Glenda, by her side The Woman and Kathy began to maneuver the planchette. Patsy wanted to know the name of the man she would marry. The pointer was very slow but finally spelled out Marmaduke. That sent everyone into gales of laughter. They were still giggling when Kathy asked where she was going to live. The planchette was still sluggish. It moved around in circles and then spelled out Limaperu. They decided to have Sandy and Kathy operate the planchette. The Woman asked if she was going to be wealthy some day. The pointer zoomed over to NO. Sandy then put some candles on the box to use for projecting shadows on the stone wall. They joined hands and were silent for several minutes watching the weird effects of that. The Woman noticed that Glenda was slumped over on her mother's arm.

Then Glenda sat up, "I dreamed I saw an owl."

Sandy and The Woman looked at each other.

Just then a breeze blew through the tree above and acorns fell down on top of the cellar. They heard an owl hoot from a tree across the road.

"Okay kids, we're done for tonight." Sandy said as she began to gather things up.

"Yes, I think it is time for some hot chocolate and cookies; blow out those candles and let's go in." The Woman said as she stood up. The kids were ready to go in the house to join Brian and Ellie in front of the television.

Sandy and the girls went home the next day. The Woman and Kathy carried the chairs back to the house and brought the candles in.

"Wasn't that weird how Glenda dreamed about an owl and then we heard one?" Kathy commented.

"Yes," The Woman replied, "that did seem strange." That was all The Woman would say about it.

The Regression
1976 - Huntsville, Arkansas

The Woman was sitting in the kitchen having coffee with her friend, Ellie. They were waiting for Delores Cannon, who had asked The Woman if she was willing to be regressed back to a former life.

Years ago The Woman's Aunt Mina had read her palm. Since then, because The Woman had expressed an interest in the paranormal; her aunt had sent boxes of books and pamphlets about everything from UFO's and E.S.P. to volumes on Edgar Cayce. Even though The Woman had her doubts about previous lives, she was curious. Mrs. Cannon told her to have a friend come and sit in during the session, and she would be taping this for her records. She said she might write a book sometime on the subject.

Soon there came a knock on the door. The Woman

and Ellie went to greet her. They discovered that they already knew each other because Ellie had a sandwich shop in town where Delores ate sometimes.

Delores got her recorder out, it was a clumsy portable but that was probably all that was available at the time. She wanted The Woman to lie down on the sofa and to get a pillow if she needed one to be comfortable.

"I am not going to hypnotize you, but try to lead you back to a previous life. Try to remember to keep talking and talk loudly enough that we can hear you. The first thing I want you to do is to go back to your childhood home and stand in front of it."

That was easy. The Woman loved that big old house and the shady yard.

"Next I want you to float up to a cloud up above you." She paused for a moment."Now float down and tell me where you are."

The Woman began to speak, "There is a boy, about thirteen years old wearing ragged clothes coming down off a ship. He is running along the beach toward a city. Many of the buildings have red tile roofs."

Delores encouraged The Woman to go to a later date.

"There is a man wearing a three-piece suit sitting at a drafting table. He is drawing plans for things such as lanterns for the captain's cabin and other accessories for a ship builder. His office has bay windows overlooking the harbor. The windows are framed in beautiful wood work, polished mahogany. The view of the seaside village is sunny and the sky is a clear blue. He is putting on his overcoat and hat and leaving the office. He is walking along a street paved with bricks."

The Woman sat up then. She remembered everything she had seen, but that was the end. She asked Delores if she would like some coffee, but she said she had to go. She thanked the two women for their time.

After she left The Woman asked Ellie what it sounded like. She said, "Your voice sounded like you were far away, I doubt if the recorder picked up all of it. Do you think this was a previous life?"

The Woman laughed, "I have no idea, but it was interesting. I did take mechanical drawing in school and it was a class I liked. But more than anything I couldn't get over how impressive the wood around the bay windows looked. "

Years later The Woman saw several books by Delores Cannon on a shelf in a bookstore. They were all studies of the Prophecies of Nostrodamas. It is likely she could not assemble enough information for a book on reincarnation. Delores had moved to California from Huntsville, Arkansas.

Out Of Body Experience
1974 - Arkansas

After school started, and the kids were out of the house, The Woman began taking naps in the afternoon. This seemed to help her cope with the arthritis that had been bothering her while she was at work in Kansas City. She seldom experienced pain in her arms any more.

One afternoon she lay down on the sofa dragging the crocheted throw over her body. She gazed at her feet enclosed in white socks and her tan pants sticking out from the throw as she lay there thinking about what she was going to do the next day. She immediately fell into a deep sleep.

When she heard the sound of tires on the gravel driveway, she jumped up.

She turned to arrange the throw onto the back of the

sofa. When she touched the throw, she realized it was warm and there was a body there. She looked down saw the tan pant legs and white socks from under the throw. Then as quick as a wink, she had returned to her body. She woke up then to see her feet at the bottom of the sofa.

The Woman sat up and thought to herself, *What just happened here?*

She had read about people who claimed to have had out of the body experiences, but she wasn't convinced that such a thing was possible. Perhaps this was just a dream.

Ten minutes later, The Woman heard the sound of tires on the gravel driveway. This time she was awake. The Man came in the back door carrying his thirty five pound garment bag and his overnight bag. He put them down at the dining table and threw the trash from KFC into the waste basket. "Come here and give me a kiss."

The Woman wrapped her arms around his neck and they stood there smooching for a few minutes.

The Man looked at the clock, "What time does the school bus get out here?"

"Not for another couple of hours," The Woman answered between kisses. "Nothing like a little 'afternoon delight'."

Later he dressed in his overalls and t-shirt, "Since I was coming back from Memphis there was no use for me to go on to Kansas City this afternoon."

"How was your trip to Florida?" The Woman asked as she was straightening up the bed.

"Well, you know I meet a lot of guys at these Central States conferences." He said as he stood in the doorway watching her.

"Frank Sheeran always invites me to this restaurant he goes to in Hollywood, Florida. This one guy took me out on his yacht. Then we sat around their table where they hang out. They always put everything on their tab. That guy gave me a phone number to call if I ever have any trouble with anybody."

As he was speaking he had that little smirk on his face that The Woman hated. As he turned to go out he said, "Well, I guess I'll go see if I can get that tractor started."

The Woman took in all this information with a grain of salt. She had learned not to take everything he said as gospel. Hollywood, Florida didn't sound like a very impressive place.

She watched the clock while she started supper to make sure she was at the bus stop on time. After the long ride from school, the kids hated walking up the hill to their house. They were the first kids on the bus, in the morning, and the last ones off after school. They were gone for almost nine hours and they were starving by the time they got home.

Cougars, Bears and Road Runners
Arkansas

The Woman walked back and forth in the kitchen cleaning up the dishes from breakfast. The kids had left on the school bus to go fourteen miles to school. They lived in Madison County, Arkansas, closer to Kingston than Huntsville. The home was situated on the side of one of the higher hills in that area. Some called it Brother Adams Mountain and some people had never heard it called by that name.

When The Woman went out to the back yard to feed the big black dog, she could hear chain saws over on the next hill. She hoped the new people who had bought that property were not cutting down the Pine grove.

On one of her walks through the timber she had discovered the big area of Pine trees. The rest of the property was covered with rocky ravines and Oak and

75

Hickory trees. It was the second growth – most of it had been clear-cut years ago.

There was a lot of brushy undergrowth and briars, but The Woman enjoyed walking through the woods anyway. She stood looking out the window at the nearby pond and wondering if she should make a trip into town for groceries. Suddenly a huge bird flew down, landing on the dam. The Woman went to the window to see if she could identify the bird. It looked like a crane or some large water bird. While she was trying to find her bird book it flew up. *It must be a Sandhill Crane*, she thought. Then she saw the reason the bird flew away. Down the path from the hill came a mountain lion. It was strolling along on the way to the pond. Behind was a young one bouncing along, jumping this way and that, like something out of a Disney movie. They stayed at the pond, pouncing here and there. The Woman was stunned to see them appearing almost to be playing. It was about ten o'clock in the morning. Suddenly they were gone. The postman drove by and that is what frightened them off.

The Woman thought the reason the cougar was moving around was because of the woodcutters working in the area. The Woman knew no one would believe that she saw a Cougar even though she had heard locals telling about seeing them. She went out after waiting awhile to see if the cats had left any paw prints. They had not stepped in the mud around the pond. Then she heard a loud screech. Black Dog had disturbed the young mountain lion and it ran and leaped up a tree. The Woman hoped the mother was not close by, as it was already too late to run. But evidently the older cougar had moved on. The Woman went over to the tree to look closely at the young cat. It snarled at her then jumped down and ran into the weeds.

The Woman wrote to the Arkansas Conservation Department but never heard back from them. She read in several publications that there were no mountain lions in Arkansas or Missouri.

The Woman was also surprised to see road runners in this area as she thought they were only found in the southwest. While she waited in her truck for the school bus to drop the kids off she would often see the road runners darting here and there among the weeds at the side of the road.

The Arkansas Conservation Department brought black bears into the hills during the 1970's. The Woman wasn't thinking about this when she went out walking with Black Dog. As they were strolling along through a tall grassy area a fairly large animal zoomed past them and ran to a pile of brush. She and the dog had walked right by it and even the dog didn't notice it. When she told Clyde about it he said it was probably one of the black bears that had been turned loose in the area. Later she saw a very young bear in a tree near the house. It was probably hungry. The Woman didn't think the woods offered much for a bear to eat. Much later in the fall when she was washing dishes The Woman saw a very large bear standing upright at the edge of the field.

The first few years after The Woman moved here she walked alone through the woods, down into the rocky ravines and even over on Clyde's land. Now, even with the dog, she was beginning to have second thoughts about this and kept more to the roads and closer to home.

Turkeys and Turnips
Arkansas

The Man's Uncle Clyde decided to raise turkeys in one of his poultry houses. He lived a short distance from Brother Adam's Mountain where The Woman and three children lived. Clyde was seventy-four years old. He walked with a flat footed gait setting each foot down solidly to make sure of his footing. He had done hard work in his lifetime, and he was still working. He knew how to run this poultry operation.

He took care of the baby turkeys, making sure no water leaked out on the floor of the building. Kathy and Terisa helped out at first by walking slowly through the building to keep the little turks from huddling together which would cause them to smother.

The turkeys grew very fast. Soon they were too large to stay in the poultry house. Clyde had about an acre of ground suitable to graze the turkeys. He erected a low fence around this area.

"Piney," he said to The Woman, because that is what he had begun to call her, "if I made the fence any higher the turkeys would fly over it. But if the fence is low they will stay inside. Tame turkeys are some of the dumbest birds there is. If it rains they will hold their heads up and drown because the water will run up their noses. It's a fact."

Next came the operation of herding the turkeys out of the house into the pen. Clyde had every kid helping as they herded small groups at a time to the pen. Clyde was herding the kids and the kids were learning how to herd turkeys.

Meanwhile, The Woman was staying away from this operation. She was making elderberry wine, canning green beans, and reading her Foxfire and Mother Earth books to see what else she could try.

The next time Clyde had time to have coffee with The Woman, he told her that the turkeys would eat every blade of grass, every stick, and every small pebble off the ground where he had them penned. He said that when the turkeys were picked up he was going to sow grass seed and a half pound of turnip seed on the ground where the turkeys were. And that is what he did.

There was plenty of rain that fell on the seeds. In a short time Clyde had a big field of turnips that were nearly as big as footballs. Clyde told The Woman to go get as many turnips as she wanted. They were the best turnips they had ever eaten.

The Woman began searching through her Mother Earth book for a recipe she had seen. There it was; a recipe for turnip kraut. She had a big crock that her folks used to make kraut in and she went to work.

The kraut tasted better than The Woman thought it would. But she couldn't keep it at a regular temperature, so she was reluctant to can it like the recipe said. Some of these things her folks used to make were kind of tricky. She would never make it if she had to do things the way the old timers did. She would have to stick with making jelly with powdered pectin and buying store bought chickens.

Clyde's turnips lasted well into winter even though he shared them with everyone he knew.

One Dog, One Chicken, Two Ducks and Two Geese
Arkansas

The Woman had become acquainted with two women who lived a mile from her house. She had mentioned that it might be fun to have some ducks to swim on her new pond by the house. Susan told her she had two geese and two ducks she would give her. Susan told The Woman the birds were kind of wild so whenever she and Leanne could catch them they would bring them to her. Somehow the gals caught the ducks and geese. They put them in sacks and let them loose on The Woman's pond. The Woman had the mistaken idea that the geese and the ducks would stay around the vicinity of the pond.

In reality they stayed in the yard near the dog. As they walked around eating grass, the geese were chortling and making noises as if they were talking to each other. Ducks and geese would all go to the pond for an occasional swim.

The next to arrive were twenty five chickens Bill bought. Until he could build a pen and shed for them, he put them out in a little building with a fence around it meant for hogs.

The next morning when he came to look after the chickens, he found them all dead except for one. His own dog, Rowdy, had come back and killed them during the night.

The Woman took the chicken that was still alive to the yard where oddly enough it stayed very close to Blackie. Now, The Woman had one dog, two geese, two ducks and a chicken.

In the spring the male duck, which was much larger than the female, began mating very aggressively with the little female. She didn't seem like a domestic duck; unlike the others, she would fly back and forth to the pond. The Woman figured this mating procedure was normal, until it seemed that the male duck was after the little one all day long. She felt sorry for the female but didn't know what she could do about the situation. One afternoon she looked out just as the little female walked out of the yard. She never came back.

The male duck was beside himself. He tried mating with the chicken, but that was a joke. Then one morning The Woman noticed there was only one goose in the yard. A fox must have gotten one of the geese. She had never put them in a pen or a shed. Now her livestock was dwindling. The duck was happy though, and he had begun to trail along behind the goose the way her previous partner had.

A week later while The Man was cutting wood with the three kids helping (which delighted the girls so much The Woman had to hear about it for the entire next week). The Woman heard a noise down at the pond across the road. She went to look and there was the gander she thought had been caught by a fox.

She called to him and he began running up to an opening in the fence. Then she understood what had happened because here came the duck running toward the gander in hopes of keeping him out of the yard. Just then The Man came striding in the door with the girls straggling behind and the boy carrying the chainsaw.

"Hurry and get your gun," The Woman cried out. "That crazy duck is chasing the goose away!"

Always happy to show off his marksmanship, The Man had the shotgun loaded and dispatched the duck in a flash. "You want to cook it?"

The Woman shook her head, after the experience with plucking chickens she wanted no part of that again. "No, just take him out in the woods and let the coyotes have him."

During the following week the geese seemed different in some way. The Woman realized that although they were walking together, the geese were not "talking." After a couple of weeks the geese began their normal chortling.

The drama was over until The Black Dog decided to adopt a nest of baby rabbits. There were things about living out on the mountain that The Woman didn't care for. That big dog trying to take care of four baby rabbits was one more thing.

Cash Reunion
1974 – Arkansas to Warrensburg

There was to be an event at The Woman's parent's house. The Cash Reunion would be held at the home of Archie Lewis and Emma Jane Cash in Warrensburg, MO. Archie was a retired rural mail carrier. Emma and Arch together had managed a small farm and raised five children. The reunion was unusual because all five of their children attended. Normally there would not be more than two visiting at one time. These were some very eccentric individuals who had probably never been together as adults. Listed by birth order, the siblings were: Betty Caldwell, who lived with husband James. He was the mayor of Concordia, Mo. Betty sang at weddings and funerals along with other church work. Anna Samplo lived with her husband, James Henry and son Steve in Garden City, Michigan. Henry was a retired auto worker, Anna was a secretary. Their son Eric, who worked and lived with his wife in Michigan, did not attend. The Woman who lived in the Boston Mountains in Arkansas with daughter Kathy and son Brian, married to The Man who was president of Teamster Union Local 498 in Kansas City, Kansas. Two of their daughters, Linda and Terisa were living in Kansas City and would be there for the weekend; James Archie Cash, a bachelor who taught music in Alaska; Kenneth Earl Cash taught Russian, and mathematics in Alaska was married to Sandra.

The Woman and two children packed their things and were anxious to go to the reunion. The Man dropped them off in Warrensburg on his way to Kansas City where he worked.

As they got out of the car, Archie welcomed them with his special greeting. "Come in and look out."

They grinned at him and went in as he held the door open. The kids went straight to the kitchen to see their grandma. The Woman stopped in the living and dining area. James A. was standing at the table stirring sugar and milk into a mug of coffee. Anna was sitting on the sofa with pen in hand and a notepad on her lap. Kenneth and Sandy were outside watching two cousins hanging Mickey Mouse balloons from the trees.

The Woman looked at Anna. Anna smiled vaguely. The Woman thought she would get a warmer reception than that, since they were best buddies forever and wrote to each other every week. James A. was not saying anything either. The balloon hangers came straggling in and were milling around.

The Woman decided they were all suffering from jet lag. Well, she had pick-up truck lag. But, she went to the kitchen and began to wash dishes.

Suddenly there came a disturbance and The Woman heard Archie say, "Come in and look out." Patsy and Holms Beebe who were friends of The Woman had come by to see Archie and Emma. They were not aware of the big reunion. Everyone was glad to see them as they were like family. Holms cornered Kenneth; they had been in college classes together. Patsy and James A. were having an animated conversation about the Anchorage opera. There was a sudden burst of laughter. Anna began to scribble in her note pad.

Kenneth grabbed his pen and note pad out of his shirt pocket and said, "What was that, I missed it?"

The Woman wondered if she should go get her pen and pad out of her purse.

James A. proceeded to repeat the last four minutes of conversation word for word. "And also I don't believe in all this notebook foolishness. Besides I left my notebook someplace."

Linda was hanging over Anna's shoulder copying her notes. The Woman had seen this at times when maybe only one brother or one sister was visiting. But seeing every one with their notebooks did something to her. She felt like she had crossed over a line into another universe. She stared in disbelief as everyone in the room was waiting for someone to say something worth writing down. At this point, Mother came in and asked, "What are you all doing? Having a Quaker meeting?" The Woman remembered that this note-taking thing started when someone decided the family needed to document the folksy sayings and childhood stories, from the farm. Mother Cash threw these out from time to time.

Meanwhile, just as quickly as they came in, Patsy and Holms slipped out, Father had taken his book to a back room to get some peace and quiet, and Mother went in the kitchen and began rattling some pans.

There was normally much joking and wise cracking when they got together. Father was an educated, well-read man. He had a witty, droll sense of humor. Mother, had recently asked to be called Jane, saying she had never liked her first name: Emma. The parents' humor was passed on to their five children.

There was the possibility that Mother's brothers, George and Alfred might stop by. They couldn't say two words without cussing. These two old bachelors were just full of it and added fuel to the foolishness that was constantly going on. Relatives and friends seemed to have an uncanny sense that Arch an Emma had company and they would show up unexpectedly.

Food was an all important item and in spite of everything, a meal had to be put on the table three times a day because it had always been like that. There were many trips to replenish the groceries. Every time the car left the property, at least four people piled in to go. They behaved, at times, like children just let out of school. The trees had been decorated. There were lawn chairs outside to encourage people to stay out of the small kitchen. One incident reminded them that they were all fortunate to be together once again. Kenneth and The Woman happened to be in the kitchen with their Father who was losing his eyesight and mistook a bottle of rubbing alcohol for Karo syrup, which he was in the habit of drinking from time to time to boost his energy. The Woman quickly reached out to him and said, "I don't believe you want to drink that." She then took the alcohol to the medicine cabinet hoping to prevent that kind of accident from happening in the future.

Ken picked up a big western straw hat off the table and said, "Supper is on me tonight." He passed the hat around collecting money for what was supposed to be his treat.

He and Sandi, accompanied by The Woman, Brian, and Steve, piled into the car. One boy was twelve years old and the other was thirteen. Upon entering KFC Steve tripped Brian sending him careening over a chair and knocking the table over. It looked like a scene from a brawl in a western movie.

Sandi quickly straightened up the chair as The Woman and the boys picked up the table. Sandi said, "Sit down boys and behave before we get kicked out."

As they sat down Ken took his hat off, which was where the money was, and told the girl at the counter "We had a good day at church today so give me that big bucket of chicken."

To his disappointment the girl didn't even blink, but set about filling his order. The Woman knew The Reunion had started.

The next few days were spent primarily by shopping for food, preparing food and eating. Other activities were scouting for yard sales, used book stores, and wandering around in Walmart. There were several trips out in the country to visit aunt and uncles.

The house sat on five acres. There was a lot of mowing and tree trimming to do. This meant also that they had a bonfire going continuously. So there were hot dogs and marshmallows to be cooked along with hamburgers on the grill. The two boys had an air pistol to shoot at targets. Mother and Father Cash had a big garden and lots of flowers, a grape arbor and a big mimosa tree by the driveway.

Soon, The Woman and the others were running out of cash - there were plenty of Cashes but no cash. At this time none of them had credit cards or debit cards. It was not easy to cash out-of-town checks. James A. announced he had a friend at one of the banks who would cash their checks. Anna, Ken, The Woman and Jim got in the car and went to the bank. The Bank was remodeling, so they had to park in the back parking lot. They walked across broken pavement and around stacks of lumber to get to the back door. From there they walked down a long hallway to his friend's office. James A. introduced them and they began getting their checkbooks out.

"Oh no," Anna exclaimed. "I brought the wrong checkbook."

Ken reached to his shirt pocket where his checkbook should have been, "I don't have my checkbook." He said with a blank look on his face.

The Woman was digging around in her purse. She finally looked up, "My checkbook isn't in here."

It was usually James A. who pulled such stunts and now he was totally abashed by this turn of events. There was nothing to be done but to make the long trip down the hallway and out to the back parking lot and go to the house. When they arrived there Mother Cash told them that Father had found The Woman's checkbook and taken it to the bank. So they got Anna's and Ken's and went to track down Father. After finding him the group went back to make the trek to the office in the bank. When they finished their transactions Anna commented, "Well that was par for the course." Anna, The Woman, and Ken decided it had been worth the ordeal just to see the look on James A.'s face.

Soon people were packing up to leave. Linda and Terisa were driving the Alaskans to the airport. Anna and Steve were leaving before the weekend to drive to Michigan. The Woman, Kathy and Brian would stay until The Man came to take them back to Arkansas.

When the family arrived at their Arkansas mountain home they were tired from the long trip. They began unpacking and changing clothes.

The Man came into the kitchen holding his size

thirteen boots out for The Woman to see. "Both of these boots are full of corn! Look at your boots. They are full of corn."

The kids started bringing shoes and boxes out of their rooms. Everything that would do for a container had corn in it.

Before they left they had brought the bags of corn for the hogs inside so varmints couldn't get into them. But a pack rat had come in the house and worked very hard storing up corn in everything in the house except the kitchen cabinets. Evidently it couldn't get in there. But it had stored corn in the bathroom and other rooms. The Woman was shaking corn out of things for weeks.

The Man got the dog to come in the house to see if the rat was still in there. He opened the doors and it wasn't long before the rat came out of hiding and flew out the front door. The Man patched the hole that he assumed was where the rat came in and they were not bothered with it again.

Trucker's Annual Christmas Party
1974 - Arkansas

The Man had been president of Teamster Local 498 for a year. The Woman had seldom visited him in his office in Kansas City. She gathered from what he told her that things were going well.

Apparently he represented men who had been fired or were having disagreements with a company. It was said that he infuriated one lawyer so much that the lawyer ran out of the courtroom and threw his briefcase a half a block up the street.

Well, The Woman believed that if The Man was at the Pearly Gates, St. Peter would eventually throw his halo down and yell "oh hell, go on in!"

The Man traveled a lot. He seemed to be on his way to Chicago, Dallas, Mississippi, or Washington D.C. quite frequently. More and more often he would not be able to come home for two weeks and sometimes he would be gone for three weeks. The Woman seldom heard from him during the time he was gone and she would not contact him unless it was an emergency. She was usually busy trying to keep things at home on an even keel.

Early in December, The Man came home on a Thursday instead of Friday evening. He told The Woman that the truckers over in Springdale, Arkansas were having their annual Christmas party Friday night. He represented these men, and they invited him and his wife to the party.

The Woman thought maybe this party might not be as boring as some they had been to, but no matter, it was assumed that she would go. She did have suitable clothes on hand as it would be more casual with a country and western band. There was always plenty of food and drinks available at these dances. However, she still wouldn't know anyone there.

On the drive to the party The Man talked about his trips to Washington. When he told her how much they had to pay for a single meal she was amazed; that was more than she spent in one week on groceries for the family. He liked going to Biloxi because they had great seafood and catfish there. He said he would like to take her there sometime.

When they arrived at the big warehouse that had been cleared out for the party, they could hear a recording of Patsy Cline singing, "Walking After Midnight." There were already a few couples on the dance floor. He maneuvered around through the groups of couples to pick up some cokes and paper cups to take to a table. A few of the guys stopped him as he made his way to a table. He had brought his own bottle as he did not drink beer. He poured some coke and a small amount of Jack Daniels into a cup for The Woman then fixed a stronger drink for himself. He sat with his back to the table so he could look out on the dance floor. The Woman sat at the side of the table watching the dancers and The Man. The live band was coming in while a couple was cutting it up to "Blue Suede Shoes." Then the band got things rolling with a hot rendition of "White Lightning." The band was good, and their singers were good, also, which The Woman was thankful for. The Man showed no sign of joining in the festivities. He was content to sip his drink. He got up occasionally to get more cokes and ice which he would swirl around in his cup.

After a few minutes, one of the drivers stopped by their table. He shook hands with The Man, spoke to him and The Woman, and moved on. In between "Don't come home a drinkin' with lovin' on your mind" and "I can't stop lovin' you" another fellow came by. He shook hands with The Man and spoke to The Woman and moved on. The Woman observed this behavior being repeated throughout the evening. At one point a portly man dressed in a three piece suit followed by a younger carbon copy of himself stopped in front of The Man. He introduced his son to The Man and stood there asking

The Man for the favor of helping with a job for the son while "Six days on the road" played in the background. The Man said he would look into it.

As this scene unfolded The Woman realized that the men were paying homage to her husband. The Woman was stunned. The music was becoming too loud and there was a larger crowd on the dance floor. She had a strange feeling in the pit of her stomach. She felt that she no longer knew who he had become. He had attained a position of some power, and he wanted her to see this. She was glad when he decided to leave.

The Woman was in a daze as they drove through the dark crooked roads to their house on Brother Adam's Mountain, but this time it was not caused by Jack and Coke. She was thinking about what happened that night. Then she began thinking about what she could fix to eat when they got home, because, even though there were tables loaded with food at these gatherings, The Man would hardly ever touch any of it. The food having been prepared by people he didn't know in kitchens he hadn't seen and set out on long tables was not appetizing to him. Besides, he knew The Woman would fix him something later at home.

Laundromat
1974 - Huntsville, Arkansas

Brother Adam's Mountain was fourteen miles from Huntsville. It was the normal thing to go into town twice a week to get groceries and wash clothes. She packed the family's dirty clothes into two duffle bags and a basket then threw the bags in the back of the truck and put the basket on the seat in the cab of the truck and started off to the laundromat in town. She had one boy still in school and the daughter was a dentist assistant in town. Her husband was working four days away and was home on the weekends.

When The Woman pulled up in front of the Laundromat she could hear Berta who was already well into one of her monologues. The Woman was acquainted with her because she had seen her at the school their daughters both attended.

Berta was a tall sturdily built woman. A striking

woman, in spite of the fact that wisps of her dark hair had come loose from the way she had it tied in the back with a scarf. She was wearing a huge mustard colored sweatshirt and some baggy slacks. She was talking to a woman across the washers on the other side of the room.

"You knew Darlene and that Arlie took the baby and went off to Arizona? Well, he was lightin' a boiler and blew hisself to kingdom come. I was glad. He thinks nothing can happen to him. He thinks he's one of God's chosen ones. He thinks he can't get hurt or sick, but I guess he knows now he can. I told Henry and the kids I was going out there to be with Darlene; they all went mad, absolutely mad. But I told them it was my daughter and my money and I would go if I wanted. But that crazy Henry said he'd burn the house down if I went. He is getting crazy.

You know, after a woman gets to be thirty-five she doesn't want sex as often. And now when Henry hollers and yells at me to go jump in bed with him I say no. Then he calls me a hormone sexual. That's green! That's real green to call someone a hormone sexual. Henry just isn't up with the times - the world is changing - he ought to go join up with that Anita Bryant. He don't know things are different now. I'd rather he'd call me a son of a bitch than a hormone sexual. One of these days I'm going to pack my stuff and I'm going to leave them all. Henry is getting crazier all the time. He's teaching the boys foot fighting. All they do is foot fight and he's teaching them to talk down on me. All but Darrell. Darrell just sits back and watches them and don't say anything. Darrell said would I take him if I go? Someday I'll just take Darrell and just leave this place and Henry can go ahead and burn the house down."

The Woman went out to her truck and found a scrap of paper to write this speech down. At the time she thought of it as being humorous. Later when she found this among her papers she realized it was a profound statement of that time.

The Boston Trip - Hoffa Disappears 1975

The Man was going to be in Boston for an International Teamster Conference so he wouldn't be home for two weeks. July twenty-ninth would be their wedding anniversary, but The Woman, unlike most women, did not make a big fuss about this date. Oddly, The Man was more likely to bring a gift of some kind and be more sentimental about it. It was also his birthday, but he became angered if she got him a gift. If she did anything it was to bake his favorite pie. Since he was going to be gone neither of them mentioned it.

Clyde came up to the house on Tuesday. "Piney, every year we get together with some of the neighbors and have a picnic down at the house. We fix it up for the kids to play some games and have races. Judy and her family usually come from Tennessee. We are going to make two batches of homemade ice cream. William and Pat cook hot dogs and hamburgers on their grill. So you all and Ellie and Bill need to come on down. Tell the kids they can bring their fishing poles if they want. They can fish right out there in front of the house. Tell my nephew we may have our machine fixed so we can shoot some blue rock."

"He isn't going to be here Saturday as he has to go to Boston, but we'll be there. I'll call Ellie. Maybe she can cook some of those blue rocks for us. I remember a woman asking me one time how to cook them because her husband told her he was going out to shoot some."

Clyde laughed, "If anybody could cook blue rock it would be Ellie. See you later, alligator."

The Woman began making a list of things to get at the grocery store. She would make a salad and a cake for Saturday. She knew Ellie would fix potato salad and lots of other good stuff.

Thursday on the 6:00 o'clock news it was announced that Jimmy Hoffa had disappeared. There were already many theories as to what could have happened to him. The Man was among many who were considered to be "Hoffa men." There were several phone calls for The Man from people who were not aware that he was in Boston.

Saturday when they went to the picnic the adults were talking about Hoffa's disappearance. The kids had a good time. Some of the younger men got them organized to play ball and race around the big pond. It was too hot for much activity. They took turns turning the crank on the ice cream maker and as the sun was going down it was time for the ice cream and a variety of cakes. The Woman was impressed that this group of people could get together. They were scattered around the area and hardly ever saw one another through the year.

The following Friday when The Man walked in and began talking before he even put his luggage down. "I don't know anything about the disappearance of Jimmy Hoffa! I don't know why people think I know anything about it."

The Woman raised her eye brows at this as he seldom came in volunteering information.

He rambled on "I don't know why they think Chuckie had anything to do with it. The F.B.I. follows those guys they are accusing around all the time, so when would they have time to do something like that. Chuckie used to be in Kansas City. Roy Williams introduced me to him. I have worked with Holms on car-hauling contracts. It was his car they say Chuckie was driving. And Provenzano had a big party for all of us on an island outside of Boston. We had a good time in Boston. One of the taxi drivers took us all over town to see the sights. We saw a replica of one of Columbus' ships, the Boston Harbor, the old church, and he took us everywhere. Then we went out where Tony Pro had a big party going."

The phone rang then. The Woman heard him say he didn't know. Probably the government had him killed.

Several people called. He would tell them Hoffa was probably killed because he had a new book he was working on. Finally, he told The Woman to answer the phone and say that he was outside. He left a pile of pamphlets from Boston on the table and a souvenir from the conference. It was a replica of a silver plated Paul Revere bowl with an inscription and the date. The Man seemed to have really enjoyed seeing all the sights on this trip.

He left then to go into town to get gas for the tractor and see Bill. The Woman put the silver bowl back in the box and put it in the closet. There wasn't a shelf or cabinet where it could be displayed. She put their supper in the oven. She sat on the front porch hoping for a breeze to come her way. Brian had gone swimming with Calvin and David. Kathy was in town helping Ellie. The Woman looked out over the hills thinking it was too bad this chair didn't rock. The Man had never sat on the porch and relaxed. He was a restless man and had to be moving all the time or watching television. She was glad he took the truck to town to get gas. She hoped it would act up for him so maybe he would buy her a different truck with new tires.

Brian Goes on an Adventure
1975 – Arkansas

By this time, The Man's army buddy, Smitty, from Wisconsin and his wife and their six children had moved to Berryville, Arkansas. When The Man had invited them to come for a visit a year ago, they went back to Wisconsin and sold their dairy farm in order to move to Arkansas. Berryville was thirty miles north of Brother Adam's Mountain, so the families visited fairly often.

Also their friends, Bill and Ellie, had moved a mobile home onto the property next to where The Man and The Woman lived. Brian and Bill worked together and Brian liked being around the couple. Ellie usually had something good to eat for starving boys.

One lazy morning in June there was not much going on. Kathy had gone to town with Ellie. Bill had gone to Kansas City. While The Woman talked on the phone to her mother, her son was throwing dish towels, socks, pencils, and whatever he could find that was handy at her. When she hung up the phone she gathered it all up and threw it back at him. Then she went out on the front porch to look at the view before going to work in the kitchen. By this time Brian, who was now eleven years old, had ridden his bike up the road and back. He rode over to the porch.

"I think I'll ride to Berryville to see Smitty and Sam."

The Woman discounted this and asked, "Where is Ted this morning?"

"Oh, he had to help his grandma today." He said as he rolled his bike back and forth.

The Woman went in the house to snap some green beans. She might have enough to can today.

While she was canning green beans Brian was pedaling his little bike six miles on the rocky hilly road to the highway. About two miles along the highway the bike broke down. It began to rain, but he was determined to go to Berryville. A man driving a church bus gave him a ride to the point where he was turning off the highway. The boy walked on.

After The Woman took the jars out of the canner, she went to the garden to pick tomatoes. Then she began to think about what to cook for supper. Kathy and Ellie came back from town. Then The Woman thought about Brian. She hadn't seen him since that morning. She called around the neighborhood and no one had seen him. She called Ellie and told her she believed Brian must have gone to Berryville on his bicycle. She called Smitty and Donna at Berryville. One of their kids answered the phone, she told The Woman that her mom and dad were not home and she had not seen Brian.

Ellie and The Woman got in her car and drove to Berryville looking along the highway for Brian. He was not at the Smith's. They started back wondering where he could be. Ellie was so worried she became ill on the way home and had to stop the car. The Woman was beginning to get uneasy, but she did not worry too much. The boy was like his father in some ways. He was in and out and eventually would show up.

But when they arrived home Brian was still not there. The Woman was just about to call the sheriff's office when Smitty and Donna drove up with Brian in the car. They had been on their way to Fayetteville when they saw Brian walking along the highway. They picked him up and took him with them and now were dropping him off at home.

The Woman could not be angry with the boy, because, after all, he told her where he was going. When The Man came home the next weekend, he took Brian to see if his bike was still in the ditch where he left it. They brought it home and patched it up although it wouldn't last much longer.

Brian and The Go-carts

After Brian's attempt at riding to Berryville on his bicycle, Smitty invited him to come and spend a night or two with them. The boys had some go-carts and a track to race them on. The Woman took him there in the truck and said she would come back in two days to get him.

Kathy was staying with her friend as they were going on a Walkathon from Huntsville to Withrow Springs. She was catching a ride with Ellie to come home in the afternoon.

The Woman spread her watercolors out on the table, made a pot of coffee and intended to do nothing that day except paint. She hadn't had any instruction on the basics of watercolor painting. She became very frustrated at times, but she enjoyed trying to paint the view from their hill.

When she was painting, she was completely engrossed in it.

Suddenly the ringing of the phone jarred her out of her deep concentration.

"Hello?"

The voice on the line announced, "This is the Carroll County hospital. Your son Bobby is here in the emergency room and he seems to have a broken arm..."

The Woman spoke up quickly, "I'm sorry, but I don't have a son named Bobby. And my son is in Berryville right now. Oh no! Wait! I do have a son named Bobby, but we call him Brian. Is it Brian?"

The Woman hurried to get dressed wondering all the while why some of the Smiths didn't call her.

When she entered the emergency room she couldn't believe her eyes. There sitting on the very sterile white table was Brian. He was covered from head to foot with black tarry dirt from the go-cart track. His eyes and mouth were the only places on his body that were not black. After she signed papers and gave them insurance information the doctor had his wrist x-rayed and put a cast on his arm. The doctor told her he had broken bones in his wrist. "And by the way, we washed his arm first."

The Woman wondered how he would ever get clean. But after they got home she wrapped his arm in plastic and he managed somehow to wash his hair and take a shower.

Kathy Graduates
1976 - Arkansas

Kathy was an honor student. She went to school every day except when she and Terisa had the mumps. She always had her school work done because this was just the type of kid she was. She belonged to the pep club which meant The Woman had to drive in to town at night so she could attend football and basketball games. Living so far out of town caused problems with Kathy's social life. The Woman didn't like going to ball games, but she also didn't want to drive back home only to return after the game. So, she waited in the truck reading a book as there was nothing else going on in town.

When Kathy turned fifteen, The Woman was hoping soon Kathy would be able to drive to the games. For some reason Kathy kept failing the written driver's test. The Woman couldn't understand why this was happening. Why wouldn't she be anxious to begin driving? Unlike other parents, The Woman wanted her to begin driving to the ball games. Finally, she passed the written test and The Woman began letting her do her practice driving on trips to town. She had been driving in the field by their house but not on the road. The first time out she drove into a ditch on a curve. As they progressed, The Woman realized that Kathy had trouble steering around a curve. Not turning a corner, but rounding a curve. So they went to get glasses. The optometrist said she was nearsighted in one eye and farsighted in the other eye. Now maybe they could drive down the road without going into the ditch. When Kathy could finally take the truck out by herself, the steering wheel came loose as she was driving down a hill. Luckily she kept her head and was able to stick it back on and keep on driving.

When Ellie opened the café in town, she hired Kathy to help out. Kathy was a good worker and enjoyed staying in town after school and on Saturdays.

By her senior year she went to work as a dental assistant. The dentist talked about the possibility of her taking courses to become a dental hygienist.

When Kathy graduated, The Man and The Woman were both in attendance at the graduation. The Woman had missed Linda's graduation and Terisa skipped out of her graduation.

Kathy intended to continue working for the dentist and stay at home and save her money for a car. But this plan went astray. One day when The Man was at home on the week end, Kathy got a phone call from her friend Janet. While she was on the phone, The Man kept saying "Who are you talking to?"

He asked The Woman "Who is she talking to?"

The Woman frowned at him and said, "I don't know."

When Kathy hung up the phone, The Man asked her who she was talking to. She didn't answer him.

He asked The Woman, "Don't you want to know who she is talking to?"

The Woman answered, "It's none of our business who called. She is working, she is seventeen years old." Besides, although she wasn't going to tell him, she knew it was probably Janet.

The Man shook his head as if he couldn't understand this concept. After he left the room The Woman realized that in his family the parents continued to try to keep control their children even after they were grown. Not that anyone could exercise any control over him.

Kathy wasted no time finding a place to rent in town. The Woman was not sure anyone would rent to someone that young, but Kathy found a trailer she knew she could afford. The Woman helped her move in. The Man didn't understand this either, but there was nothing he could do about it.

Brian and Ted
1972-1979 - Arkansas

It was nine-thirty when The Woman sat down to have another cup of coffee. The phone rang. A man with a deep voice said, "Just a moment, your son needs to talk to you."

Oh no, The Woman thought, *They are finally going to kick him out of school for some of his shenanigans.*

Brian's voice came on the phone, "Hey, can you bring me a shirt. I'm in welding class and my shirt burned right off my back?"

"Well, are you hurt? Do you need to see a doctor?"

"No," he replied, nonchalantly, "It's just my shirt got on fire and singed my hair a little."

The Woman got dressed and drove fourteen miles to school to give him a shirt.

The winter of the big snow, school was not in session

for a week. Brian and his friend Ted had a wonderful time. They tromped all over the fields and woods stopping at neighbor's houses wherever they thought they would be fed. They rolled snow into a huge ball. When The Woman went out to take pictures of it she got snowballed for her effort. So she took pictures of the boys throwing snowballs at her. They spent the evening playing board games while The Woman baked cookies and made hot chocolate.

One night Brian and Ted had been at Bill and Ellie's, talking. It was very dark out. As was The Woman's habit, she went out on the front porch to look out across the hills. When she looked up the hill toward Bill's house she saw two lights swirling around. She knew it was Brian and Ted, but what could they be doing? It almost seemed like they were dancing. She watched until the cold air chased her back in the house. She sat down and began reading her book. Then she heard the boys come up on the porch. The two red-faced boys came in. They began pulling some things out of their jacket pockets. Meadowlarks were soon flying all over the house and scurrying under the furniture. There were at least fourteen Meadowlarks they had caught. The Woman could only think about these birds getting under the beds and dying in the house. She told the boys to catch every one of them and put them back outside. Later, she read that the birds normally got under the snow into the grasses. But the snow crusted over and these birds got shut out. Hopefully the boys disturbed the snow enough that the birds survived.

One evening in the fall Brian and Ted came in to get Brian's shotgun. He had owned a gun since he was eleven-years-old, as many hunters' sons did. He and Ted had spotted some ducks on a pond someplace. They walked down the road until they could see the pond. Then they crawled until they were close enough to shoot. It was almost ten o'clock when they came back to the house. The ducks had been dressed and were ready to be cooked. The boys wanted to know if The Woman would cook them. She told them she would. She had some cornbread and enough fixin's to make dressing. So in the middle of the night the boys sat down to a duck dinner.

Brian seemed to never get enough to eat. The Woman could buy him a cheeseburger and milkshake in town. He would be eating a ham sandwich as soon as he got home and asking her when supper would be ready. One night, for a snack, he cooked six eggs, seven pieces of toast, and drank a quart of milk.

Brian and Ted became obsessed with the idea of playing a prank which they must have seen in a cartoon. It was the old purse trick. In the cartoons it was usually played in town or in a residential area where there was a sidewalk. The perpetrators would tie a string on an empty purse and when someone stopped to pick it up, the perps, who were hiding behind a bush, would pull the string yanking the purse away from the victim. The boys were growing into men and they talked about the purse trick every waking hour of every day. Every time The Woman thought they had given up on this, she would hear them talking about it again. She told them it was not very likely they could pull this off out in the country because people were driving and wouldn't see the purse. They said they had already tried this in town. A woman got mad at them and told them to go home. Eventually, The Woman forgot about their obsession. They had both been working. Brian was helping Bill with a fence and Ted had to help his grandmother. Then one evening, it was getting dark, when The Woman realized the boys hadn't been by to get something to eat for awhile. She called, but Bill said they were not there. The Woman didn't know why, sometimes she had a sixth sense about things, but she got in the truck and drove down the road toward Bollinger's Store which was five miles away - where the road joined a county highway. She drove through the night not really thinking they would be down this road. But when she got to the highway she began laughing hysterically. The headlights on her truck picked up a web of fishing line crisscrossing above the highway. The line went across from an embankment over to some fence posts and back again. No doubt there was a purse lying in the middle of the highway. Soon the two boys appeared out of the darkness and crawled into the truck. The Woman couldn't talk for all her laughing. This was one of the most comical sights she had ever seen. She backed the truck around to head home. Ted said, "One old drunk guy kept driving back and forth. He was trying to figure out what that was." The Woman thought the old guy may not have been drunk.

Hogs, Secrets of The Rock, Visiting With the Artist: Willy Radke June 22, 1978 - Arkansas

Wednesday, The Woman went out to the hog pen to feed the hogs and check on one of the sows. That sow was due to deliver a litter soon. When The Woman looked into the pen she realized the big event had begun. Raising pigs was an idea thought up by The Man and Bill. The Woman went back to the house and called Bill. Neither of them knew much about raising hogs. The Man had gone to work that day. By the time The Woman and Bill got to the pen, the little pigs were shooting out like link sausages. He seemed to think the little ones should be picked up and put in a cardboard box which they did. When it was certain that all the little pigs had been born, Bill coaxed the sow into the shed and took the pigs out of the box. Then he shut the door so the little pigs couldn't get out. Later they checked on the sow to make sure she had plenty of water and food.

Thursday, The Man called to say that he had to go to Kansas City over the weekend. If The Woman wanted to go with him to pack a bag as they would probably go by and see the two mothers in Warrensburg and spend the night.

The Woman packed and bought some easy to fix food for the two teenagers who would be staying at home. One had a job and the other had football practice. They would be alright while she was gone unless they killed each other.

Saturday after looking at the little pigs, The Man was ready to leave. They drove along at a pretty good clip until they got to Highway 71 and then he drove really fast. The Woman kept her eyes toward the scenery out the side window. This way she could be more relaxed as he sped along pretending not to be racing with the other cars. He said he had to stop at Harrisonville to pick up something for the tractor. He also knew an old boy that lived here so he wanted to see if he was at home. He bought a little bolt like thing at the tractor place. His friend was not at home, so they went on into the city. He drove to the union hall to see someone there while The Woman sat in the truck. Then they went to make an appointment to get bed liner sprayed in this new truck. Just as The Woman thought she would perish from hunger, he stopped at a bar and grill for sandwiches. The Man ate very fast, but was content to talk to some men in the bar while The Woman ate. The men always had to say, "I see you brought the boss with you." And, "Say, that's not the gal you brought in here last week." The Woman always laughed as if she hadn't heard this a dozen times or more. When he started jingling his car keys, The Woman took another sip of coffee and let him know she was ready to go.

He then zigzagged across the city to a The Blue Moon Lounge, "I want to see if Danny is here this afternoon."

The Woman was amazed to see the inside of the lounge was done up in royal blue and the horseshoe bar lit up the sparkling crystal. The outside of the building didn't give a clue as to what was inside. The manager came to greet The Man then took The Woman's hand and kissed it. The Woman almost jerked her hand away thinking, "I wonder what he would think if he knew I was in a pig pen delivering pigs with that hand." But she tried to act civilized about it even though she had only seen this done in the movies.

Maybe I have been in Arkansas too long, She thought.

The Man bought them both a Jack Daniels and Coke as they sat at the bar. He talked to the bartender and the manager. Then he went to the restroom. He saw some people at a back table he knew. He ordered another drink for himself. In a few minutes Danny came in. They slapped each other on the back and The Woman got introduced.

The Man told Danny that Robert and some guys were at the back table. They both got up and walked back, stopping momentarily about halfway there to talk.

In the meantime three men who were dressed in smart looking suits came in and sat down at the bar. The bartender introduced them to The Woman. They were lawyers from an office near the lounge. One of the men spoke to The Woman, "I heard about the bass you caught, did you have it mounted?"

The Woman had taken the kids fishing at a local pond with cane poles. They had hoped to catch enough perch for supper. When they got ready to leave she discovered she had a fish on her broken cane pole. When she pulled it out there was a twelve pound bass on the line. Her ten-year-old son had been ecstatic. They had taken the fish home and the boy set to work trying to clean the fish as he had seen his father do. It never occurred to them that a fish was worth anything except food. Since then The Woman soon learned that this was a trophy fish.

She grinned as she answered the fellow at the bar, "No, we cooked it and ate it." She loved the expression on men's faces when she told them that, knowing they wondered how this woman could be so ignorant.

The Woman felt her husband's hand on her shoulder as he spoke to the lawyers. After talking to them a few minutes The Man was ready to leave.

The Man then drove to his mother's house. They stayed there a few minutes and then went to visit the other mother. The Woman stayed with her mother. After reading the newspaper, The Man left to go see who he could see in this town.

Sunday morning The Man and The Woman left to go back to Arkansas. He told her he knew this guy who was an artist. He said Willy Radke had learned air brushing while he was in Alcatraz. "Maybe you would be interested in that kind of art since you have been painting."

"Sure," The Woman told him, "I'd love to see his paintings." *And*, she said to herself, *how often does a person meet someone who has been Alcatraz?*

The Man said he was going to stop at the next town at a bakery because they baked German black bread that was "just like they used to bake in the old country."

After stopping at the bakery they drove to a small town off the main highway. They stopped at a two bedroom cottage where there was an old model green Packard sitting in the driveway. The people there seemed glad to see The Man. Willy, his wife, Louise, and his son were there. Two of Willy's paintings hung on the wall above the sofa. They were both scenes from the southwest; probably done from photographs. They were good paintings, but they were not discussed at length. The Man mentioned that he was going to work in Joplin soon.

Willy Radke was a small wiry man in his late seventies. He seemed energetic and very sharp. He handed the book, *Robbing Banks Is My Business* by Harvey Bailey to The Man.

"Here's that book I promised you. Oh, you know I used to live in Joplin."

His wife interrupted and corrected him, "No, you used to hide out in Joplin."

They all laughed at that.

Willy said, "Yes, I was hiding out in Joplin back in the late thirties and forties. The boys had an apartment where we would hang out when things got too hot in Kansas City. Sometimes we would leave each other notes, "See you in New York or see you in Chicago."

The Man said he used to know an old boy who had been a guard at Alcatraz.

Willy said he knew some of those guys came from Missouri because they talked like hillbillies, "They would say 'bresh' instead of 'brush' and things like that."

It was getting late so The Man and The Woman said goodbye to the Radkes. Soon they were back on the main highway and headed on toward Arkansas.

Years later, The Woman was watching a television show, "Secrets of The Rock-Return to Alcatraz." It was about Alcatraz and had some of the former residents on the show, including Willy Radke.

Brian Starts His First Business

As Brian was leaving the lunchroom when he was in the sixth grade, a teacher asked him if he would help pick up the milk cartons that were left on some of the tables. The punishment for leaving a milk carton was that a student had to help pick them up. Since Brian did not leave his, he told her "no."

She then said, "Oh, be a good Christian and help out."

He replied that he was not a Christian and walked out. The Woman was surprised when he told her what he had done as he was usually a helpful kid. But since that was a punishment she guessed Brian didn't think he should have to do it. And the remark about being a Christian didn't set well with The Woman who didn't like the fact that most people assumed that everyone was of the Christian belief or that only Christians were good people.

The Woman received a call from the principal the

following week. One of the teachers had seen Brian riding around town in the morning, before school, with two girls.

The Woman thought to herself, *So what?*

But she asked him what the problem was. She told him that the boy's sister had driven to school and he rode with her.

"Well," he whined, "Brian has been buying bags of candy at the store before school and selling candy to the other kids at recess and that is against the rules."

The Woman told him she had advised her daughter to let Brian out near the grocery store so Kathy could avoid the morning traffic at the school.

"But I will tell him to stop selling candy." *Which*, she thought, *you could have done in the first place*. She hoped the good Christian teacher was satisfied now.

She wondered how much Brian made off of his business.

Brian's High School Years

Brian was a good athlete. In the seventh grade his coach made a plan to see if his losing team could win at least one game. He switched Brian in the middle of the game from tackle to quarterback because Brian could throw a pass. It worked. Brian was a football hero. He was selected to escort the Homecoming Queen.

He played football and baseball in high school. The Man said he was a good football player. The Woman went to the games, but they made no sense to her. She would rather see a baseball game. One day in the grocery store The Woman heard an announcer say her son's name. The store had the replay of the high school football game on a TV. The Woman didn't get this channel out on Brother Adam's Mountain. She had no idea the football games were replayed on TV. In another store when she wrote a check for something, the clerk commented, "Oh, are you Brian's mother?" The Woman had no interest in football and when she had gone to her son's games, he seemed to be doing nothing but knocking people down and they would all stand back up just to get knocked down again. She didn't realize that so many people followed the games. *So,* she thought, *first I was my father's daughter, then my husband's wife and now I am Brian's mother.*

Then his wrist was broken. It was a bad break and took him out of football his senior year. Then another boy broke his arm. The coach told Brian sometimes he just felt like crying. Brian said he knew the feeling. After two and a half months, the doctor, who treated the Razorback athletes, finally took the cast off and told Brian to keep his arm in a sling for awhile. That night a boy attacked Brian while he was sitting in a car with the door open talking to someone. Jasper was angry about something Brian had said and ripped the sleeve off his football letter jacket. Brian managed to kick him off without using his arm and the driver of the car took Brian home. The Woman was outraged that Jasper would attack someone whose arm was in a sling; especially since it had taken so long to get it healed. She called The Man, although she never called him when he was in Kansas City. The apartment manager said he would tell The Man to call when he came in. After she talked to The Man she wished she hadn't called as he had been out drinking. He told her he would see Jasper when he came home. She hoped that Jasper wouldn't come to any harm then. The next morning she went to see a lawyer about getting Jasper to pay for the jacket. He reported the incident to the sheriff's office. When The

Woman talked to a deputy, he said Jasper was a trouble maker and he would bring him in and put him in jail if she wanted to file charges. The Woman sensed that the deputy was too anxious to go give Jasper a hard time so she refused to file charges and she left it to the lawyer to get the money for the jacket and let Jasper realize he should not jump on someone who is not able to defend his self. The Man went to talk to Jasper but he said Jasper was a small fellow. To The Woman's relief, The Man did not do anything drastic.

The Woman took Brian back to the doctor. The x-ray showed that his wrist was okay, but the doctor smiled and put a new cast on. It was getting close to baseball season. Eventually the cast came off and the doctor told him he could play baseball.

In spite of dyslexia, his clowning around at school, and never bringing a book home, Brian graduated.

He had worked in the hay fields and at the turkey processing plant loading trucks. He hunted deer and fished. He was the only one of the kids who went to the proms and school dances. The Woman had a better truck by this time, and he had a car. The Man helped him buy a green Ford LTD and Brian paid for it by working at the turkey plant.

The Man and The Woman went to his graduation which was held in the gymnasium.

The Man went back to work on Sunday afternoon. When The Woman came home from the grocery store the following Monday, Brian was gone. He left a note saying he was leaving. He left the only gift he had to give. He had placed his cap and gown from his graduation on the table with a note, "To The Queen of Queens." The Woman had expected him to leave sometime, but maybe not so soon. His friend Ted had joined the navy. Brian had a hearing problem so he couldn't sign up. He went to his grandmother's house and worked for his aunt and helped his grandmother, as Terisa had done before she went on to Kansas City.

The Man was very unhappy that Brian had left; he thought he would stay out on that mountain. *And do what?* The Woman thought. She liked it there, but didn't expect the kids to stay. Actually, there was no reason for her to stay there either.

The Man said they would have to move closer to Joplin where he was working.

Linda Visits
1980 - Arkansas

The Woman and The Man had listed the property with a real estate dealer in Huntsville. The Man was going to be in Florida next weekend. The Woman started going through the items she would take when they moved. She could pack up things she didn't use and put things to go in the sale in a box. She liked to be ready to go when they found a place. The phone rang Monday night. It was Linda. She said she had a long weekend coming up and would be there on Saturday.

The Woman stopped dragging things out of the attic and began thinking about what they could do this weekend. She had some very tender venison steaks in the freezer. Maybe she would bake an apple pie. She began making a list of things to get in town. Linda might like to go to Eureka Springs and look around the shops. Linda was acquainted with Susan and Suzanne so they could visit them also. Linda would be happy just to sit on the porch and look at the scenery.

By Friday The Woman had made her food preparations. The steaks were thawing and the pie was made. She and Black dog set off down the road on one of their walks. The Woman tried to always have a plastic bag in her pocket in case she saw something she wanted to carry home. It was too late for morel mushrooms. The Woman didn't have much luck finding them any way. She picked up rocks or odd shaped leaves or flowers that she would take home. She would look them up in books to try to identify them. Today she happened onto coral mushrooms. She had just read about them not long ago and found that they are edible. Very carefully she lifted them out of the soft mossy soil. She kept Black Dog out of the way until she had a bag full of the fragile fungi. It looked like the coral from the sea. The Woman would not pick any other mushrooms because she didn't know that much about them, but she felt okay about cooking these.

She took these to the sink right away when she arrived home. She snipped of the little roots and did her best to wash them without breaking them up too badly. Now she would have venison steaks and mushrooms for Linda's supper tomorrow.

There was just the two of them there since the other kids were gone and The Man was not there. There was no other company expected that weekend. They went to Kingston just to walk around and look at the old stores and stopped in to say hi to Susan. Then they walked in the woods. They didn't see any more coral mushrooms. Things like that are here one day and gone the next. Linda loved the venison dinner.

She left on Sunday afternoon so she would have time to stop in Bella Vista and see Kathy. By now Kathy was a dispatcher for the Bella Vista Police Department.

Leaving Arkansas
1980

After Brian left, The Woman had something else to worry about. The weather had turned hot. There was no air conditioning in the house or the truck. The days passed and there was no sign of a break in the heat wave. She swam in the coolest pond every day, but she couldn't stay in the pond or the shower all the time. When The Woman went into town, she wrapped a wet towel around her shoulders.

Bill and Ellie had sold their place and moved to Alpena. Susan and Suzanne had parted. Suzanne went north and Susan went to Fayetteville. The only traffic on the road was the mailman. No one was moving around because of the stifling heat. The Woman thought about going to visit her mother but she kept thinking it would rain soon. The Woman went ahead with her packing.

The Man was now a business agent for Teamster Local

823. If they moved near Joplin he would be home almost every night instead of just weekends. Meanwhile, they tried to do what they could to make the Arkansas place presentable in case the realtor brought some buyers out. The land there was selling at higher prices than when they bought it and they had made a lot of improvements on the house and land.

The real estate agent brought two women out to show them around. One woman was a lawyer and the other was a special education teacher. They wanted The Man and Woman to finance the deal. Ordinarily they wouldn't do this, but an agreement was made that satisfied The Man. Quicker than they thought possible, it was time to have a sale and get out of Arkansas.

The weather had begun to cool down by the day of the sale. The Man dragged every old bucket, rusty chains, all the tools he no longer wanted, piles of lumber, and lawnmower into the yard. They sold most of their furniture. People around there were tired of the hot weather and were ready for a sale. The auctioneer sold everything in the yard. People had a good time; The Man's sister, Kathy, and The Woman served sandwiches and cold drinks all day.

The Man and The Woman went to Missouri to look for a place to live. They found 20 acres, a mile from Pineville, on the Elk River. There was a sandbar on the place that was big enough to have picnics. There was a huge barn and remnants of a log cabin. An old chicken house was in the back along with a small stone shed with no door on it. There was even an outhouse on the place. The house was heated with a wood stove and gas heaters. She was anxious to sell and so The Man and The Woman bought it.

PINEVILLE, MISSOURI

Moving In - Old Sheds, Log Cabin, Dynamite and Blue Water Pineville 1980

The elderly woman who sold the house and twenty acres said her husband had died ten years ago. She had two sons, but they had not done anything to help keep the place up. The huge barn was still in good shape. There were bales of hay in the loft which had to be at least ten years old. There was a small stone shed missing a door. She said her husband used to sit up there to crack walnuts. It was evident as there were walnut shells all around on the ground by the shed. In the back of the house was a garage, an old chicken house, a log cabin and even an outhouse complete with a quarter moon shape cut out on the side. Before they tore it down Brian and Linda each had their picture taken walking toward the outhouse.

The move was relatively painless as The Man and The Woman had sold most of their furniture at the sale. The Man was working in Joplin at the Teamster local as a business agent. He had vacation days he could take so he used them to work on the property. He and The Woman started cleaning up the area right away. He mowed weeds and set about burning the chicken house and the outhouse. They cleaned out the garage and a friend of his came with a paint sprayer and painted it. He walked along the river and clipped the huge vines and trimmed tree branches. There was a sandy beach on the property. He said that would be a good place for cook outs. He began making plans to have a road graded so he could drive to the beach. The river was a different environment from what they were used to. The river changed from day to day. It could flood and change course. The river was also open to the public and canoeists could stop and spend time on the beach if they wished. The Man was not happy about this.

The Woman saw an ad for someone wanting to buy logs from old log cabins for a restoring project. The log cabin on this property had vines growing over it and was so unstable neither The Man nor The Woman dared to enter it. So she called and told the person they could have any good logs provided they help burn the rest. It was too bad it had to be torn down, but it was a hazard. The fellow brought his son to help and the four of them spent

Saturday morning taking the cabin apart. He loaded several logs on his trailer. While they burned the rest The Woman said she was going to go get some cokes for everyone. The Man asked the fellow and his son if they would like some moonshine in theirs. They said sure. So the four of them sat out there to watch the fire and drank moonshine and coke out of paper cups. The next day after the fire had gone out and the ashes had cooled The Woman raked through the ashes. She found an old whiskey jug that had apparently been under the floor of the cabin for over one hundred years. It was in perfect condition and even had a corncob stopper in it.

The Man had to go back to work the following week. The Woman began cleaning house. It was nice to be only a short distance from town. She went in and bought cleaning supplies and went to work. She put lots of blue stuff in the toilet stool and cleaned everything in the bathroom. Then she went to the kitchen and began work on the shelves cleaning and putting shelf liners in the big kitchen. Then she noticed something very strange. There was blue water coming out of the faucet. She knew immediately the septic tank was seeping into the well. The following week she was subjected to the noise of drillers as they drilled a new well. At least The Man was there to deal with it.

Several weeks after the excitement of the blue water, The Woman took a hoe and an old broom up to the stone shed by the side of the road. She began scraping and sweeping off the bench where the old man must have sat while he was cracking walnuts. She swept the cobwebs down and wondered who had built this and what it was used for. Outside she began sweeping the walnut shells and leaves into a pile. She should have brought the rake with her. She was scraping around with the hoe when she hit something in the ground. She dug awhile with the hoe then gave up and went to the garage to get a shovel and a rake. She dug all around this thing with the shovel. She dug a big hole until it was about two feet deep. She recognized this object to be a chicken feeder like some her mother used to put in the brooder house. It was the type that held the feed inside a galvanized tube and the lid slid over it to keep the feed dry. The feed fell down into a tray as the chickens ate it. The Woman tugged at this feeder until it came loose and she was able to pull it out. She pulled up on the lid but it was rusted to the tray. She took the hoe and banged all around the lid until she could gradually pull it off. Inside she saw seven tubes wrapped in white with the word Dynamite written on them. She had never seen dynamite. There was a glass jar with something in it also. The Woman thought, *If this is over ten years old it could be very unstable.* Unstable or not she couldn't leave it there. She went to call the sheriff's department right away to see what should be done with it. A deputy came and very calmly carried it all to his car. "I'll take this out and when I'm burning some brush I'll throw this on the fire," he told her. The Woman was amazed that he would put this in his car and drive off as she expected it to blow up at any moment. When she told

The Man what she had found he said, "I could have used that." No one seemed concerned that she was beating on the chicken feeder full of dynamite with a hoe.

Flood
1981 - Pineville

Linda had plans to visit. The road from Pineville along the river was flooded, but Linda found the back road to her parent's house. She and The Woman watched as the little stream rose until it was even with the lawn. They had been assured that the river wouldn't get as far as the house and that proved to be the case. Never-the-less, it was eerie to watch the power of the flooding water.

"Oh, good grief!" The Woman called out to Linda. "There goes a dead cow. Oh, I hope that cow doesn't get caught up in some brush on our property. Can you imagine what that would mean? How awful, I can't believe the flood would be so bad that a cow would drown." They watched as the cow swirled around in the rushing water. The Woman breathed a sigh of relief when it became apparent the cow had been swept away.

"Look." Linda pointed out the window, "There goes

another one and there are logs jammed up so you are going to be stuck with this cow."

The Woman got on the phone to see what should be done about this situation. Nothing. No reports to be made, no one wants to hear about the cow or do anything about it.

The cow landed at the end of the property. The Woman avoided this area all summer. One day after the weather had turned cold she went to investigate. There was hardly anything left of the cow's body. The skull was fairly intact but surprisingly few large bones were still in the area. She used a stick to pick up the skull and carried it up to the house. There it lay on a table outside all winter. Eventually she cleaned it with soapy bleach water and Linda took Lucky, The Cow's skull to her apartment.

Fertilizer
Spring 1981 - Pineville

The Man suffered from allergies the year around and had long since lost his sense of smell. The Woman complained often about the odors from a nearby hog farm, but he didn't have a problem with that. She had to keep the windows closed when the wind was blowing from that direction.

The Man had found out from his many sources of information that fertilizer from this hog farm could be had for pastures for a very low cost. A truck would come from the hog farm and spray it in a liquid form on the grass. This sounded like a good deal to him.

The truck came and sprayed. The Woman began closing the windows and spraying room deodorizer all over the house. The Man was standing by the back door nonchalantly watching the fertilizer truck.

The Man watched until the truck left. When he

stepped inside, The Woman called out, "Whoa there, buddy, you can't come in here with those clothes on. Take everything off and throw them over those bushes. Then you had better go take a very long shower. I don't know if that smell will ever come out of your clothes."

The neighbor across the way saw The Woman in town the next day. She came up to her and said, "The first day this spring I could open my windows and your husband had to have that obnoxious stuff sprayed on his pasture."

The Woman lamely explained that her husband could not smell it and had no idea how bad it was.

The Man Working In Joplin
1981 - Pineville

After the move and The Man's vacation was over, The Woman found that things with The Man were much like they were when she lived in Arkansas. He was still traveling to Dallas, Chicago, Kansas City, Springfield, and Florida just like he used to. She had their meal ready by five-thirty. She soon learned to eat her supper and put his in the oven. When he was working in Joplin he didn't come home until late at night. He evidently started drinking during happy hour when he got off work and would hang around The Rafters with his friends until late. Not only that, but he was stopping to drink at a lounge on the highway near the house and at The Judge's Saloon which was also nearby. She had been waiting for him to come home and he was right up the highway from their house. If he wasn't out drinking he was watching television. The Woman didn't care much for television and she didn't know his friends very well. When they went out she couldn't drink much and would just sit at the bar and read bar signs until he decided to go home.

The Woman went back to her painting and making quilts. She joined an art group and learned more about watercolor painting.

Terisa and her two children had moved to Arkansas but the kids in Kansas City came to visit more often as it was a shorter drive than the Arkansas place. Kathy was working in Bella Vista, Arkansas. Since that was just a short distance, she and the Woman could go shopping and visit quite often. Sometimes The Man would take them to a lounge called Ginger Blue for margaritas and dancing whenever there was a band playing. It was very nice to be living so close to several towns for a change.

After Frank Fitzsimmons died Roy Lee Williams was quickly installed as president of the Teamsters Union (International). The next Central States Conference was going to be held several months later in Chicago. The Man was going to drive there. The Woman asked him if he could take her as far as St. Louis so she could visit her Aunt Mina and pick her up on the way back. He agreed to do that. When they got to her aunt's house The Woman's cousin, Wendell, took them to the VFW for a drink. When they returned to Aunt Mina's The Man told her that he wasn't coming back through St. Louis so The Woman would have to go on to Chicago with him. The Woman never knew what was going on in The Man's head, so she didn't question their change of plans.

On the way to Chicago, they met other teamsters who were going to the conference. They spent the night at a motel and drove into Chicago early the next morning. They checked into The Ramada Inn at O'Hare airport. Right away The Man said he had to go see Roy. The Woman bought some post cards and went out to sit on a bench to address the cards. She went to their room and began to read a book. She stayed there until The Man came. They ate lunch, then sat at a bar where several men were watching the Cub's baseball game. The Woman noticed there were men standing in groups around the lobby area. Most of the men were dressed in the same type clothes. They wore slacks, short-sleeve dress or sport shirt, and dress shoes. Some of them had the large belt buckles with the Teamster logo on them. These were union officials. There were a couple of clusters of men wearing business suits. They were the lawyers. They had come for the conference and had nothing to do but stand around and wait. A man sitting across from them at the bar was trying to get her attention. She realized that he had no way of knowing she was there with her husband as The Man was busy talking to someone on the other side. She was doomed to keep her eyes on the ballgame so as not to make eye contact with the guy. She finally was able to poke The Man in the side and told him she wanted to go back to their room.

Later, The Man came to get her again. He said Roy would be coming down soon. The other men were gathering in loose groups on either side of the hall.

While they were standing there a nice looking woman in a blue business suit came over to The Man and began asking him if he would like a tour of Chicago. She said she would like to show him around. She said she was there for a meeting also. She tried her best to get The Man to go with her. The Woman was laughing at his discomfort. She figured some of the other men there had paid this classy prostitute to come to put him on the spot and maybe to see what his wife's reaction would be. After all, there were over a hundred men there and she zeroed in on one man.

Shortly after the prostitute left, Roy Williams, his secretary, and others in his entourage came walking down the center of the hall. When he was almost even with The Man and The Woman, he veered off his path. He walked over to The Man and shook hands with him. The Man introduced him to The Woman even though she had already met him. He shook hands with her and introduced her to his secretary, Billie and to the other men. He then continued his walk to the auditorium.

The Man and The Woman went to eat after everyone had gone to the meeting. He told her he didn't need to go because he had already seen Roy. But after they finished eating he walked with her to their room and he went on to the meeting.

The next morning The Man drove through Iowa to Missouri stopping only for gas and sandwiches. He was used to driving long distances and when he got on the road the miles flew by.

After The Woman was home from Chicago, Kathy began to spend more time in Pineville. She was working at Bella Vista, Arkansas which was only a short drive. When she got off work at midnight sometimes when The Man was out of town she would drive to Pineville. She and The Woman would drink wine and play Scrabble until three in the morning.

They went shopping the next day or walked down by the river. If The Man was at home they would go to a bar called Ginger Blue and drink margaritas. Linda came to visit more often since it was much closer than the place in Arkansas. One night they were walking to the river and she heard the heron's harsh call as it flew over. As they sat by the river in the moonlight they heard an owl call out. Then another owl answered. It was very pleasant to be walking along the river at night.

Firecrackers and Whisky
1981 - Pineville

Mixing Firecrackers and
Whisky Can Be Risky

When The Man came back from Dallas he installed a gas heater in the upstairs living room.

The heat from the wood stove in the lower level wouldn't circulate up to the second floor. The Woman had seen an article in a magazine that explained this. The fellow who wrote it had cut a hole in the upper floor and ceiling of the first floor and installed registers so the air could circulate. The Man was not interested in this piece of information so now he had a gas heater to warm the area around the television set.

The next day he went to Springfield, Missouri. The Woman went to the grocery store and later walked to the river with the dog. The rest of the day she painted a watercolor scene. She cooked smothered steak and put some of that in the oven for The Man as he would probably be late coming in.

At nine o'clock the phone rang. It was Agnes and Jeanie from Springfield who, were the wives of a couple of men The Man socialized with at a club there.

Agnes started off with, "We are at the hospital with your husband. A firecracker went off in his hand and we are waiting for a surgeon to come and take care of him."

The Woman broke in, "Wait a second, do you mean to say he had a firecracker in his hand? He is absolutely against anyone messing with firecrackers."

Jeanie came on the line. "We are calling you because we want you to know what happened before he talks to you. He and the guys have been sitting over here drinking all afternoon. Then tonight they started lighting firecrackers and dropping them into a glass of water before they went off. He got one with a short fuse and it went off in his hand. We know how these guys are and we wanted you to know what really happened."

Agnes got back on the phone. "We are going to bring him home when the surgeon finishes wrapping his hand."

The Woman had met Agnes and Jeanie and she told them she appreciated the phone call. In a few minutes the phone rang again. It was The Man. "Hello, I'm waiting for the surgeon to come and doctor my fingers.

Somebody threw a firecracker down on our table and when I went to brush it off it exploded and messed up my hand. These guys are going to bring me home."

The Woman replied, "Agnes called and told me what happened."

The Man interrupted, "Well, she doesn't know; she wasn't even near our table when it went off. We'll be over there pretty soon. Bye."

When they brought The Man home, Agnes told The Woman that he had a shot for the pain, but it was going to wear off and it was going to be very painful. He was supposed to keep his hand elevated. He was strolling around and took the men out to see his new dog. The Woman told Agnes they could stay, but if they were going back to Springfield maybe they should go so he would settle down.

Yep, he had plenty of pain. The Woman went to a local doctor he had seen for allergies and begged for a strong pain medication. The prescription she gave The Woman didn't help much. When he was able to sleep she turned the phone off. He watched TV and read books.

The Woman believed Agnes was telling the truth about the accident because The Man never showed any anger toward anyone else causing it. She knew if someone else had thrown the firecracker that would be a horse of a different color.

He had to go to Springfield after four days so the surgeon could change the bandage. He drove, of course, and dropped The Woman off at her friend's house before going for his appointment. On the way home he said the doctor gave him the things he needed to change the bandage. He had to soak it then slip the gauze sleeves over his thumb and forefinger. The Woman would have to help him. He went by the union hall and they said they had two hundred calls about the accident. The favorite among the rumors was the one where a union rep was blown up by plastic explosives.

The next night he took The Woman to The Shangri-La for drinks which The Woman needed after the harrowing job of helping change the bandage on his fingers although he managed to do most of it himself.

Texas Relatives
1981 - Pineville

The Man and The Woman had moved to Pineville several months ago. Now Mary and Jess, his sister and brother-in-law, were moving to Rogers, Arkansas. Kathy was moving from Bella Vista to Fayetteville Arkansas. Terisa had moved back to Kansas City. Joy, The Man's sister, was in Warrensburg and she moved on a regular basis from house to apartment and back to house. His mother decided to move to Rogers, Arkansas to be near Mary. Linda had recently moved from an apartment to a house.

Since The Man had already moved, he became restless and decided he and The Woman would take a trip to East Texas. He liked to visit his cousins; he had fond memories of the summers spent there working on their truck farm, fishing and hunting. Cousin Bondese and Aunt Bessie lived in the original house that had been built on the property fifteen miles north of Jefferson, Texas. On the circular drive five hundred yards from that house was the house that Cousin William and Phyllis lived. A little way from there was a new house that William's son and wife were living. William was retired from The Texas Highway Department and Phyllis worked for Social Services in Jefferson. Cousin Lugo and his wife lived in town, but he still had his house on the circular side road near Aunt Bessie's. He was in the fur business buying pelts from local trappers and selling them to fur buyers. He had these pelts hanging on a line over by his house.

The way they had their houses together on the same property was due to the dividing of the land by John Mott years ago. John Mott had farmed many acres which he divided among his boys. Each one had built a house on the place. William and Bondese raised watermelons, okra, horticulture beans, purple hull peas, onions, potatoes, squash and many other vegetables. They had a vegetable stand down on the highway where they sold their produce. Many people from the area, black and white came and picked from the field. William and Bondese had a sheller that made it easy to shell all these beans and peas in back of their house.

While The Man and Bondese were out riding around, The Woman and William stayed at the house. William was watching his grandson for his daughter who worked over at Marshal in a jewelry store.

After he threw some new logs in the fireplace, he noticed a conch belt on the mantle.

"It looks like Lugo left this belt here. This here is a conch belt that the Dreesen's great uncle, Robert Lowthry cut off a dead Indian when he was with Kit Carson. He hated Kit Carson. Carson had ordered the men to retreat, but Lowthry was surrounded by three or four Indians and arrows were falling all around him. He was face to face with the chief and he killed him. The other Indians left then. Lowthry cut this belt off. It is sand molded silver discs laced together with rawhide strips. Kit Carson punished Lowthry for not obeying his command by tying him down spread eagle in the hot sun. He nearly died. Here's a picture of him when he was an old man."

The Woman looked at the picture of a man with long white hair and a long white beard. She thought this was a pretty good story. William found he had a good audience, so he continued,

"When I was bringing in those sticks of wood awhile ago, well, me and Bondese, we cut up limbs and trees that have fallen so we don't really cut down many trees for firewood. Anyway, we were down by the creek cutting up some downed limbs and here came old Zack Mott with his axe over his shoulder. He showed up two or three days before that. Zack would go live with Joe, then Will, first one and then another until he would get mad. Then he would move on. So he came striding across the field with his valise and his axe to stay with mama. He was a good hand with an axe; he could cut down a tree as fast as you could cut it with a chainsaw. He told us we were damn fools for messing around with those limbs on the ground. He said he could cut us up some fire wood a lot quicker by cutting down a tree. We didn't want to do that so he got mad and packed his valise and went off to stay someplace else. He was a prison guard down at Huntsville a long time ago. He had a club he had hollowed out one end and filled with lead. One day he saw a black guy, who was a cook, spit tobacco juice on the meat and he got onto him about it. The man came at him with his knife and Zack hit the black prisoner with his club. He killed him and they had to fire Zack. He wasn't really as mean as Milt."

The Woman remembered seeing the infamous Uncle Milton Mott in 1957 when she and their two little girls accompanied The Man to visit his Aunt Bessie. Bondese and Aunt Bessie had prepared a breakfast of homemade biscuits, eggs, bacon and coffee.

As Bondese set an extra plate on the table he explained, "Sometimes Milt stops by for breakfast. He's been doing that since Ida Mae died." They were just ready to sit down when they heard car tires on the gravel drive. "There he is now."

The door opened and in walked a slender man who was at least six feet, three inches tall. He was wearing a western straw hat, a blue shirt buttoned to the neck and at the wrists, and faded jeans. A belt with a gun and holster hung at his right side. He hung his hat on the back of his chair and they all sat down. The Woman with Terisa on her lap was seated beside him. She was careful not to let the baby touch this man. Thankfully Linda was seated between The Woman and The Man for she was more likely to be curious and always want to hug everyone.

Aunt Bessie said, "Milt, this is Charlie's boy and his wife, they are here from Missouri."

Milt didn't look up from his breakfast, "Hlo," he said. And other than a few words to Bondese he never spoke again. When he finished eating he got up and put his hat on and left. It seemed to The Woman that everyone breathed easier when he was gone.

Bondese began talking about Milt, "You Know, he's got an arsenal in the trunk of that car. He drives that car like it is a tank, drives through the fields, over stumps, if he wants to go someplace he just drives on through a creek or anything. He's got enough ammunition to fight a war. You know why, don't you? It's because he was so mean. Them coloreds had to cross the street when they saw him coming or there was no telling what he would do. You knew he shot that one? The colored man was drunk, up on the old bridge, cussing and waving a gun around. Somebody hollered, "Go get Milt!" And when that colored guy heard that he jumped in the river. When Milt come up there on the bridge he just stood there looking at the man floundering around in the water. Somebody asked Milt why he didn't shoot him. He told them he was waiting for him to get out on shore so they wouldn't have to drag the river for his body. Sure enough when that guy got up on the bank, Milt just raised his rifle up and shot him. He was just as mean to white folks. He was the town marshal and he was mean to everybody. That's why he has all those guns in his car. Scairt he is. That's why."

The Woman realized that William was off on another story.

William was saying something about Zadie's funeral. "When he died, Joe Mott and Zack went to help out with the funeral. There was a lot of the colored people out here who were good people. Everybody liked Zadie, he was good with horses and mules. People would go get Zadie when they had a sick animal. Joe and Zack loaded Zadie's coffin onto their truck and hauled him out to the Mount Zion church where the blacks had their meetings. They took the coffin inside and set it on two straight back chairs. Then the people started coming in. The Dreesens and the Motts were the only white people there. In came the black preacher from Atlanta dressed in a Prince Albert coat and a high shine on his boots. When everyone was seated he commenced to preach the funeral. It wasn't long before the preacher got carried away and began speaking in tongues. The members began to shout and dance. Roscoe, who was six feet and four inches tall weighing around three hundred pounds, began to shout and dance. Then he began to chase the preacher around the church. Reverend Puckett was getting pretty scared and was running with his coat tails flying out behind him trying to keep out of Roscoe's reach. Roscoe caught ahold of his coat tails just as Zadie's coffin fell off the chairs and Zadie rolled off onto the floor. The congregation stormed out the door. Joe and Zack picked Zadie up and placed him in the coffin. The reverend said a final prayer as the people watched through the windows from outside."

The Woman wondered how many variations of this story were told across the south.

William began preparing lunch. Phyllis would be home to eat, as would Bondese, and The Man.

Most of the talk around the dinner table was about deer hunting and such. There were deer antlers nailed to every shed and hanging on every wall. After lunch Bondese said he was taking The Man to show him where the cemeteries were then they were going to go buy some ribbon cane syrup from Walker's store.

William and The Woman went outside to sit on the porch in the sun. The little two-year old, Max, played in the sand while four huge dogs walked around him. These were deer dogs that were there to keep deer out of the fields. She had been told they could bring down a large buck with ease. These same dogs instinctively knew they had better not ever touch the boy. Sweet, mild mannered William would kill every one of them and not blink an eye.

The Man and The Woman left the next morning. The Woman was ready to go as Texas hospitality meant three huge meals of biscuits, venison, catfish, pie every day. While delicious, this made her feel like a stuffed turkey after two days. It was a good thing she was well fed because The Man liked to drive as fast as possible from Texas to Missouri only stopping for gas.

Spring of 1982
Pineville

The Woman was visiting Kathy and her friend, Angela in February. They served spiced tea and rolls. Angela and The Woman played with the Ouija Board and were asking it about potential romances for Kathy. But there didn't seem to be any romance in the immediate future. They talked about how unhappy the queen was because the London newspapers published pictures of (the obviously pregnant) Bikini clad Princess Diana.

The Man was traveling often and was actually tired. He had just came home from Mississippi and had to go to Chicago.

In March Linda called. She and her group of friends in Kansas City wanted to know what The Woman thought about having a showing of her paintings. They were presently arranging a photography show at The Artery, which was a gallery upstairs over the Foolkiller Theater in Kansas City. They would make all the arrangements and hang the paintings. The Woman was a bit surprised. She had a lot of paintings but had never considered a show, but she said it was okay with her.

"And by the way," Linda continued, "Brian and Sharon got married today. He had just had his nose operated on and had two black eyes and tape over his nose. Since Sharon is eight months pregnant it looked for all the world like a shotgun wedding."

The Woman was glad they got married before the baby arrived.

Brian and Sharon came to visit The Woman. They went to The Dairy Delight and got ice cream cones. He and Sharon played war games on a machine that was similar to the pinball machines. They went back to Kansas City.

Kathy came the next night. She showed The Woman how the planets were lined up in the night sky and the moon was shining too. She and The Woman drank Kahlua milkshakes and played cards until three o'clock in the morning. Someone had given The Man a big bottle of the coffee flavored liqueur which Kathy and The Woman loved to mix with their ice cream. The Man had another bottle that they did not care for. It was a mix of straight grain alcohol mixed with maraschino cherries. And most of the time he had a jar of moonshine in his cabinet where he kept his guns. He would show these off and offer drinks to men who were looking at his guns, even though he seldom drank at home.

The Man came home from Chicago that night and went to work in Joplin the next morning. He called and told The Woman to bring Kathy to Joplin and meet him at Red Lobster. He talked about his plans to start a canoe rental business. They went to The Rafters to have a drink and see who might be there. He introduced Kathy and The Woman to Lang Rogers. Lang was talking about Hart Benton who was a friend of his. It took The Woman awhile to realize he was talking about Thomas Hart Benton, the artist. Lang's folks had owned the newspaper where Benton worked at one time.

In April, The Woman's sister, Anna, and her husband, Henry, came to visit. Kathy was there and Howard Wilks came for lunch and to drop off some tax papers. Anna had compiled information on the Cash family history. She had made copies for everyone in the family. Kathy and The Woman helped put these together in notebooks. Kathy left to go to work. The Woman packed her things and she and Anna and Henry went to Warrensburg to Mother Jane's. The Man went on to Kansas City.

The Woman took her paintings because Linda was going to take her to Kansas City when Anna left. The Woman showed them to Father Cash. He was able to see most of them. He was in a jolly mood and told her about his trip to the World Fair in San Francisco in the early 1900's. He had worked his way across Kansas with a threshing crew and went on from there. The Woman recalled hearing Uncle Alfred telling about working every year with the same threshing crew boss. He said the boss liked the way he worked so he had the same job of feeding the bundles into the separator.

The Woman and Anna took their mother shopping and out to eat. Then they went shopping some more. Linda came then and took The Woman to Kansas City. First, she visited Terisa and her two children. The Woman always had to attend a wild tea party with Randy and Andrea. The next morning she and Linda met with the girls to talk about the art show. The Man was supposed to pick her up there. It was eleven o'clock that morning before he showed up. He said at the last minute he had to go with some men who picked him up in a Rolls Royce. He had to show them around the city since they were from out of town. He said the Rolls rode rougher than his truck.

The Man needed to stop at the office in Joplin to make some phone calls and finish some paperwork. Then they went to The Rafters and saw Lang, Howard, and Jack.

When The Man and The Woman got home they made some vegetable soup. They were watching Television when Linda called to tell them that Brian and Sharon had a baby girl named Tonya Ann.

The next day, April the 9th Anna called to tell The Woman that Father Cash had fallen and hit his head. When he fell he hit mother's leg and cracked a bone in her leg. He was in the hospital and mother had a cast on her leg. Henry went back to Michigan and Anna stayed to take care of things. The Woman went to help out and to visit Father. She cooked and took care of the house while Anna made arrangements for Father to go to a nursing home as he was not recovering well.

Early in May Linda's friends had the art show ready. They had printed a list of paintings, Linda had fixed thirty-eight paintings to be hung, and they even had wine and cheese. The Woman couldn't believe they had worked so hard on this, but it was what this group of women did. There were many people coming in all day long as it was on a Saturday. The Man had gone with The Woman to see her father and then took her to the art show. He had to leave to go to work so The Woman stayed that night with Terry and the kids. The next morning The Woman went to Pineville on the bus. The bus stopped at the lumber yard and she walked home from there.

Surgeries Broken Bones
1982-83 - Pineville

Terisa needed a gall bladder operation. The Woman needed to have dental surgery. Since Terisa needed surgery right away, The Woman made plans to go to Kansas City in order to care for six-year-old Randy and four year old Andrea. The Man was out of town; Linda couldn't take off from work, and The Woman hadn't driven in Kansas City for years. The Woman made elaborate plans in order to get there by bus. The bus stop was less than a mile from the house. After calling Linda to tell her what time to meet the bus and arranging with The Man to pick her up, when she was ready to come back, she was ready to go.

She drove her luggage to the bus stop and left it. She drove home and walked back to the bus stop, leaving plenty of time to get there before the bus arrived. She had done this once before. She had walked home from the bus stop since The Man was out of town. When she got home she found that The Man had locked all the doors when he left, and she didn't have a key. She had to crawl in a window that time.

Linda was at the bus station when she arrived in Kansas City. She had the two kids with her as Terisa was already in the hospital. Before she left the apartment she reminded Randy that Grandma would walk him to the school bus stop in the morning. The Woman let the kids talk to Terisa on the phone, then they played games, and ate supper. The Woman began reading a book that was long enough so she could read several chapters each night.

In the morning, after breakfast, The Woman made sure Randy had everything he needed for school. They walked down the stairs to the street. They walked down that block and crossed the street. They continued walking until they crossed another street. The Woman wondered about all these streets the child had to cross. The bus stop seemed quite a ways from home. Then Randy turned and started walking on a grassy area toward I-35 Highway. The Woman realized then that she had been fooled by the six year old who did not like going to school.

"Okay, Randy, "she said. "It is against the law to walk here, so we will just have to go home." He had a big grin on his face as he skipped along home. However, he did not get away with this the next day."

Terisa came home with a jar full of one hundred and

ninety six gallstones. It is no wonder she was in such pain.

The Woman was going home the next day as Terisa had assured her that a friend coming to help her. The friend couldn't come, but The Woman had already set a date for her surgery so she had to leave.

The Man was there at the bus station in Pineville to take her home. Then it was her turn to enter a hospital.

That same year Linda was in a serious car accident, saved only because she had her seat belt fastened. Fortunately she was living with Sue who looked after her and she did not have to go to the hospital.

When Anna went home from taking care of The Woman's parents, who were both laid up, she broke a bone in her foot. One of their brothers had his foot in a cast for awhile.

The Man had injured his hand with a firecracker and Brian had his nose operated on.

Seemed like nearly everyone in the family was laid up for a while.

Shotguns
1983 - Pineville

Larry and Ott were coming from Oklahoma to meet with The Man for their yearly pheasant hunting trip in Nebraska. Coming from that direction they would be on the highway across the river. The Woman could see lights from the cars when they passed at night out the dining room window as she had a habit of sitting up at night in the dark. But the highway wasn't noticeable during day light hours. She was taken aback when Larry walked in and greeted The Man by saying "Hell, man, I could shoot the windows out of your house from that highway over there."

The Woman thought this was an odd observation. She thought back to a night she had gotten up when she couldn't sleep. She returned to bed to find The Man standing behind the closet door with a baseball bat in his hand. That was quite awhile ago. Then not too long ago he jumped up out of a deep sleep, grabbed the loaded shotgun, he aimed it toward the stairs. He told The Woman he heard someone down there. She had not gone to sleep yet and told him he did not hear anything.

The Woman never bothered to lock the doors in the daytime, and knew it was not much of a deterrent at night. If someone wanted in, it would be easy to get in. She was never afraid to be alone. The Woman was not afraid of strangers breaking in; she was actually more leery of walking around the house, in the middle of the night, when The Man was home. When the escaped convicts from Kansas were reported to be in McDonald County she was not overly concerned. Kathy had called first to tell her about them and then the rest of the family called because they knew she didn't watch television. But she knew if they came to her house it wouldn't be difficult for them to break in. The Man even called, which was unusual; she told him she had heard the news. Most people would stay hunkered down in their homes but not The Man. When he got home they got in the car to go see if they could find out what the Highway Patrol and Police were doing. At one place along a highway state troopers and sheriff cars were all parked along in the same area. The criminals were caught when they tried to ride out on a train.

The closest to trouble they had was a time when they were gone and a friend's son broke in to steal liquor. The boy's father took care of that situation.

Someone loosened the lug nuts on a tractor tire. Fortunately The Man noticed this before he began mowing. They didn't know who did it; maybe the boy who stole the liquor.

Riparian Cookouts
With Elk River Entertainment
1982-84 - Elk River, Pineville

Since The Man had taken the job of Business Agent at Teamster Local in Joplin he had made the acquaintance of the other agents and people he met in several clubs. He had bought eight canoes and a trailer with the idea he might start a canoe rental. Their property wasn't really situated in a way to make this possible so he rented them out to other businesses during the height of the summer season and they used them for family and friends.

Many weekends in the summer, some of his friends from Joplin brought their campers, grills and smokers to camp out on the sand bar by the river. Everyone would float down the river to Noel. Somehow The Man and The Woman were able to go this distance without upsetting the canoe or each other. He said he would guide the canoe from the back and she would watch for logs and big rocks while sitting in the front of the canoe. She thought this was a backward way to do it, but since she didn't know anything about the canoes she did as she was told even though she doubted that she would see anything in the water in time for him to avoid it.

When they were not on the river they were entertained by the people from The Pineville Canoe rental who were floating by. A good many of them would not be able to execute the bend in the river and the cold water caused much screaming and cussing. Their coolers, clothes and shoes would be soaked and floating free of their canoes.

The Man and his friends did most of the cooking which was a welcome change from how things were in Arkansas. They came and spent a relaxing week end, cleaned up the mess and went home.

IRS
1983 - Pineville

The Woman had the room off the kitchen full of boxes they had moved from Arkansas. She had quite a mess of things in that room. Her art supplies were in one end of the counter top and quilt pieces were in sacks. She was taking things out of the boxes when she looked around at the jumble. Did she really want to sit and sew these squares together? Her quilts were just squares sewed together and not fancy at all. It was just another way to pass the time.

She was disgusted because The Man was gone all the time. The Woman began repacking their things in separate boxes. She might as well make plans to leave him. She worked at this all afternoon.

The next week a letter came from The Internal Revenue Service. It was a disturbing letter concerning an audit. It stated that because they had sold property in

Arkansas and did not buy another house they owed an astronomical sum of money. The Woman who had been given the wrong information that receipts and other tax information need not be kept after three years, had just burned a huge folder of such stuff. And where did the IRS get the idea that they hadn't bought another house? They were living in it.

The Man and The Woman went to Joplin to see Howard, their CPA and friend.

He assured them that this could be straightened out. When The Woman told him she had burned all their papers, he said, "You'll have to go to Arkansas and get receipts from every place you bought lumber and the other things you bought to fix up the place. You know why you are being audited, it's because you are a Teamster."

The Woman thought that getting people to give her receipts would be a monumental task. She disliked the idea of asking for them. She made a list of businesses she needed to see. It was surprising how open and willing people were to help. The IRS had a reputation for being unreasonable. The Woman hadn't realized this until she had been on this journey. Howard came to their house on a Saturday. He did this when he was working on their tax returns. The Woman fried catfish and fixed pinto beans with corn bread. He loved home grown tomatoes and sliced onions when they were in season. He opened up the spreadsheet showing what they needed for the hearing. He told them they didn't need to be there. Again he looked directly at The Woman and said, "The

reason they are auditing is because he is a Teamster."
He turned to The Man, "Someone who has a bone to
pick has turned you in. Even though you shouldn't owe
anything, it will cost you something and cause trouble."

It would be quite some time before all this was taken
care of. The Man was talking about moving to one of
the lakes in south Missouri. The Man and The Woman
drove around looking at Stockton Lake, Pomme De
Terre and Truman Lake on Sundays. The Woman felt
like they hadn't gotten settled in this place and now he
was already thinking about moving again.

Her plans to leave The Man got sidetracked by the
letter from the IRS. All that had to be settled first.

They stopped at The Rafters on the way home and he
told her he was going to see Roy the next day. Then he
would be going to Kansas City on Friday. They decided
to stop by and see Linda and Terisa. After visiting
with The Man's friends at the bar, they continued on
to Pineville. It was dark and rainy on the highway.
Occasionally a car would come from the other direction
and the car lights would sweep across the windshield
where the wiper blades swished back and forth. The
Man started talking. As he talked The Woman realized
this was not whiskey talk, he was seriously telling her
about who he was and things he had done and people
he knew. People she had read about in the news in New
Jersey and Chicago who were reported to be running
the unions. The Woman was shocked as she listened in
silence.

He finally said, "Oh, you don't even believe me." She did believe him she just didn't know what she could say.

He had to leave the next day for a meeting in Miami.

The Woman sat in the living room staring out the window. She wished she could call her sister, or her daughters. She wondered if their phone had been tapped. Was someone opening her mail? Was she being watched? Surely he wasn't that important in the grand scheme of things. One thing about it, they did not have any money except what he earned. She hardly ever spent money on anything but groceries. She was never concerned with his activities because she thought it didn't have anything to do with her. She sat up all night for three nights not able to sleep or do regular housework. Finally she wrote a coded letter to her sister. She and her sister often made up codes and wrote silly letters to each other. Her sister called her and said, "... and did the truth set you free?"

The Woman began thinking about things. She would not leave The Man. Maybe they would sell this place and move to a house by a lake. Possibly they could get a boat and go fishing or swimming. Things might be different when he retired. She began packing items they didn't use. She might as well not waste her time unpacking.

Christmas
1984 - Pineville

As long as The Woman could remember, her mother, Emma Jane Cash, and her father, Archie, had made Christmas a fabulous day for kids. There was the big real evergreen tree, presents for all, stockings filled with nuts, candy and fruit, a big breakfast, and a dinner of ham or turkey with all the trimmings. This was Jane's day and her children tried to be there every year except for Anna, who had decided not to fight the bad weather in December. She made her trips to Missouri in May or in the fall.

This year Kenneth and his wife and son could not come from Alaska. But Jim came every year, flying from Nome, Alaska. He would be home for Christmas if at all possible. Also Anna's son, Steve came since he had never been to this event before. Brian was living in Kansas City with his wife and daughter, Tonya. He was able to bring his daughter, but his wife preferred to be with her family for the holiday.

Terisa had to work over the holidays and was not able to come. Linda brought Terisa's two children, Randy and Andrea with her. Betty, who was the oldest sister and her husband James E., lived in Concordia, Missouri and they came on Christmas morning as did their married children; Landy, Paul, and Donna and their children. The Woman and Kathy drove to Warrensburg three days before Christmas. Kathy had days off and took extra vacation days so she could be there to help Jane shop and wrap presents and enjoy being with her Uncle Jim. The Man was to arrive later when he got off work. He and The Woman would be sleeping at his mother's house as Jane's floors were already covered wall to wall with sleeping bags.

When Kathy arrived in Pineville to pick up her mother, there was hardly room for The Woman's things in the car. Kathy had been baking cookies and making candy for a week with her friends Angela and Charlene. They must have felt like they were operating a bakery. She had boxes upon boxes of cookies and candy of all kinds piled in the car. She had just gotten off work so she crawled into the back seat with a blanket and pillow and was asleep soon after they were on the road. It was fairly early in the morning so there was not much traffic on the highway. The Woman was driving along at a pretty good clip when she noticed a car behind her. She wondered why he didn't go ahead and pass since the highway was clear. Then she realized it was a state trooper. She pulled over and rolled her window down. He informed her after checking her license that she had been going eighty miles an hour.

"Don't you ever look in your rear view mirror?" He asked. "I've been following you for quite a way."

The Woman told him she had no idea she was driving that fast. After talking for awhile and determining that it was Kathy's car, he let them go without a ticket.

Jim had wasted no time getting started on the decorating of the house. When The Woman and Kathy walked in they saw that the chrome dinette table was piled high with colorful construction paper, glue and several pairs of scissors. Amid this were coffee cups and plates with the crumbs of biscuits and jelly on them.

Kathy began bringing in her boxes of cookies.

Jane, who had been watching Jim and Steve make paper chains and wondering just how long this chain was going to be, left her chair by the window to see what Kathy had in the boxes. "Would you look at this? She has enough cookies to feed Cox's army. What is she bringing in now? More cookies? Kathy, how did you make all of this? What are these round ones. I'm going to have one of these and some coffee if Jim and Steve didn't drink it all. Did you all see what they are doing? Making a big mess I think."

Jim and Steve moved away from their project to pick out some cookies. The Woman went into the kitchen to make more coffee.

Jim said it was good they had come to help out with his paper chain. But now they needed to go to the store. Jane had a list; she wanted Kathy and Jim to pick out presents for her to give to some of the great-grand kids and a few of the grand kids. They needed more wrapping paper, and more construction paper and Jim hadn't even started his Christmas shopping yet. He liked to go to every store and look at everything and then go back and buy what he had decided on. But, he almost never got everything bought before Christmas Eve. Jim had been a music teacher and had also sung with the Anchorage Civic Opera. He was in charge of the music programs at many church functions. But when he came home he was a six feet and three inches tall child who loved Christmas as much as his mother did.

He and Steve had already gotten the tree. It was a big live evergreen. One year the trees had been sold out when Linda had been elected to buy the tree. Jane had a tall pine tree in the yard. She told Linda to go out there and cut that tree down and she would use the top for a Christmas tree. She thought Linda could do anything and it never crossed her mind that Linda could not or would not cut it down. Of course Linda cut the tree down and cut the top off. She set it up in the living room so her grandma and grandpa would have a live tree. That year the Man and The Woman, Brian, and Kathy couldn't go because of deep snows in Arkansas. The Man had to do the shopping that year and bring the food for dinner to Arkansas.

The Woman started cooking lunch which Jane had already begun. Jane told Jim he needed to move that stuff off the table. It had always been, in that house, that there were three meals a day at approximately the same time of day. It was nearing noon and so it was time for lunch.

About that time an old black Chevy truck pulled in the driveway.

"There's George and Alf," Jane announced when she saw her brothers.

Jim, Steve, and Kathy began clearing the paper off the table. Jim said to put it on his bed.

The two old uncles wearing overalls and denim barn jackets came in the door, "Howdy, Emmy." They said almost in unison.

"Well, goddamn," George said to Jim in his outdoor voice, "You came all the way from Alaska. You must have got cold up there and come down here to thaw out."

Alf broke in, "How cold was it up there when you left?"

Jane interrupted, "You all sit down here, we are getting ready to eat."

She and The Woman had opened two cans of peaches, there were some boiled potatoes and boiled cabbage ready. The Woman had fried some hamburgers and heated some hot dogs. Jane had a cake sitting on the bar. After some weak protests George and Alf sat down to eat. The Woman brought them some coffee.

George said, "I'm not like Reagan. He said he don't drink coffee for lunch because it keeps him awake in the afternoon."

They all laughed. Alf said, "I expect he sleeps most of the day, god-damn, it is really a hard job being president. Them people in Washington never did a day's work in their life."

Emma asked them if they had seen Rhody lately. They said no, but they just saw Ode over at the sale barn. Ode was laughing at Herbie. Herbie sold five hogs to Ode for fifty dollars apiece. Ode took them across the highway to the sale barn and sold them for seventy-five. Herby was madder than a wet hen.

The uncles laughed and cussed some more then got ready to leave.

Emma jumped up, "Wait, look at all the cookies Kathy made." She began selecting cookies and candy to put in a bag for them. "Jim, get those packages from under the tree. There's one for Ellie and those two cans of Prince Albert tobacco for the boys." Those six feet tall boys who were seventy-four and seventy-one years old had always been called "the boys." The brothers were off to visit Leonard and Hilda who lived in town.

After the dishes were washed and put away, Jim, Steve, Kathy and The Woman took the grocery list and the gift list from Jane. They made a list of things they thought they needed and went to town and to the new stores out on the highway. Jane was going to take a nap.

Jim had to go to every store in the immediate area.

He looked at everything from dishes to toys. Steve observed Jim in his pre-Christmas shopping operation and wondered how it worked. Last stop was the grocery store. Jim had not bought anything. The actual buying would be done on another trip to town.

After they unpacked the car and put things away, Jim went to take a nap, Steve got out his pencils and sketch pad.

The Woman asked Jane what she had in mind for supper in case it needed to be started early. Jane said she would like for The Woman to make some Swiss steak. So The Woman peeled the potatoes and covered them to be cooked later. Then she prepared the steak and put it in the oven on low. She found a can of peas in the cabinet. Then she and Kathy went to take a box of cookies and candy to her other grandmother who lived across town. They didn't stay very long there. When they returned to Jane's, The Woman sat down to read a magazine and she dozed off.

After they ate the evening meal and those dishes were washed, Jim and Steve brought all the craft supplies back to the table so the chain making could start again. Kathy began wrapping the gifts that Jane had bought. The chain was already forty seven feet long, but Jim wanted it to go all around the living room and dining area and down the hallway. Jim decided he was ready to wrap one present. The Woman and Steve watched him. The Woman took notes on how he managed to spend thirty-five minutes wrapping one gift, while Steve made wise comments as he continued to work on the paper chain. Soon they were all working on the chain and Jim began taping it up at the top of the walls. Since he was tall he seldom needed the ladder. He soon realized he was going to run out of tape. A new list was started for the next day which was alright because Jane had a new grocery list every day and Jim still had to finish his Christmas shopping. They usually went to stores twice a day at least. Jim had other decorations to put up besides the chain. The Woman knew that Jim would be wrapping presents way into the night on Christmas Eve and probably the next morning.

The Woman and Jane began assembling things for the big dinner. Jane baked an apple pie and put it away for Landy. All he wanted for Christmas was his grandma's apple pie.

Jim always went to midnight mass at the Episcopal Church. His nieces and nephews who were visiting went with him which was the only time some of them ever went to church. Then they were sorry they went because he sang in his operatic tenor voice that could be heard for miles. The kids always scrunched down in the pew since everyone in the church turned to look at Jim. Later, Jim said that Kathy nearly knocked the priest down in her rush to get out of the church.

People began to arrive. Linda sped into the driveway in her little blue Toyota truck. She had Terisa's two children with her as Terisa had to work on the holiday. She had a truck load of gifts with her. Jane was quick to go to the door and yelled "Christmas gift!" which was Jane's family tradition and no one knew what it was supposed to mean. The Man showed up soon after Linda. They weren't expecting Brian, but he came with his two-year old daughter, Tonya. Brian was determined to come to this Christmas. It was almost like everyone sensed that Christmas at Mother Cash's would soon come to an end.

The Man soon left to go visit his sister, Joy, his mother, and Curly, his step father. He came back later so The Woman could go spend the night at his Mother's house. They went to his sister's to have drinks and some sandwiches and cookies.

The next morning The Woman went to her mother's so she could try to help get everyone some breakfast and start the cooking. Soon her sister Betty would be there and her daughter, Donna A. and they could help too. The Man went back to his mother's because he couldn't stand this crowd. Soon Betty and James E. came in yelling, "Christmas gift!" They brought in food and gifts and began talking to everyone in loud voices. They exclaimed over the cookies Kathy had brought. Right behind them was Adolf, Donna A., and their two children. Betty said that Landy and his family and Paul's family would come later.

While they were talking, Kathy and The Woman were in the kitchen, sampling the noodles that Jane made every year because they were afraid they wouldn't get any if they waited.

Jim began handing out the gifts and the commotion

and noise level was wild. Somehow they muddled through this. Linda and Steve enlisted the kids' help to gather up the paper and trash. They took it out to burn it, relieved to be out of the house for a while. They dressed Tonya and took the kids over to the park and ran them around to let them use up some energy.

The Woman was in the kitchen trying to get the dinner organized. Donna A. came in and said, "I'll do that. I've helped out with so many church dinners it is easy for me."

The Woman was glad somebody knew how to get this together. She went to sit down. Soon Jane, Betty, and Donna A. had the meal underway.

In the afternoon Landy and his family came. Jane retrieved his pie from her hiding place and handed his kids and wife their gifts. After that Paul's family came by. All of them had funny stories to tell. The Man came later. By afternoon, Brian and most of the others had gone home. Things were winding down. The Man had to go to work the next day so he was leaving early the next morning. He said his mother wanted to ride to Pineville with Kathy and The Woman. She had arranged for Mary and Jess to come there and take her home with them. Kathy still had one more day to stay. She and The Woman cleaned house and shopped for groceries for Jane. Linda took the kids back to Terisa, but she would come back to take Jim and Steve to the airport when they were ready to leave.

Kathy and The Woman packed the car and went to

pick up her other grandmother. She sat in the front seat. Kathy drove. The Man's mother was a very irritating person and immediately began talking and asking Kathy personal questions. She had a habit of telling people what she thought they should do and why didn't they do things differently than they were doing now. Kathy pulled over at the next convenient spot and asked The Woman if she would drive. She said she didn't feel well. She got in the back seat and covered her head with a pillow for the drive to Pineville. She went on to her apartment then.

The Man came home after work. After they ate, his mother went upstairs to watch television with The Man while The Woman took her time washing dishes. After she finished the dishes she poured a cup of coffee, lit a cigarette, and began reading a magazine. She heard The Man's mother coming down the stairs.

"There's no use trying to talk to him. He's been drinking. He doesn't make sense, it's just blah, blah, blah. He is so drunk he doesn't know what he is saying."

The Woman doubted that he was drunk. He never seemed drunk no matter how much he had imbibed. He was probably just arguing against everything she said. But it was interesting that his mother finally saw her baby boy the way he really was. Mary and Jess were there the next day to take her to their house.

Christmas was over. Now The Woman could look forward to The Man's holiday vacation week spent watching football every day all day long. She was glad the television set was upstairs and her craft room was downstairs where she could look out the window at the river.

POMME DE TERRE

Moving to Pomme De Terre Lake
1984 - Wheatland, Missouri

The Man and The Woman were almost certain they had a buyer for the house by Elk River.

The Man was working ten-hour days, four days a week, so they had three days on the weekends to look for a place to live. They hoped to find something near one of the lakes north of Springfield. Stockton Lake didn't suit them. The Man said it was too windy on that lake for fishing. They went to the Hermitage area near Pomme De Terre Lake. It was a pretty lake with beaches and some parks. They didn't see anything very close to the lake. Another day they went on to Truman Lake which was larger.

After driving around Warsaw, Clinton, and Osceola

they went back to the Hermitage and Wheatland area. The Man drove into an area near Angler's Resort. There was a road that circled around for a half of a mile where there were several houses and a road down to a large dock. They parked on the road and looked at the lake. They didn't see any houses for sale. The Woman looked at the red house with gray stone work on the porch and balcony on the upper floor. She thought it would be wonderful if this house was for sale. A fellow came walking up the road from the lake. The Man got out of the truck and asked him if there were any houses for sale in this area. The fellow pointed to the red house and said that was his house and he and his wife had been thinking about selling it.

Mr. Hill took them right into the house. When he showed them the lower floor, his wife was down there making flower arrangements oblivious to the fact that her husband was selling their house. The house sat on lots between where the road circled so they had access to the road on both the front and back of the house. There was a detached garage in back of the house and an attached garage that was accessed from the front of the house. Best of all the dining table sat in front of a sliding door which looked out on the lake. Somehow, very conveniently all the trees had died right in front, so it was a grassy lawn across the road on the Corp of Engineers Land and nothing to obstruct the view.

The Man and The Woman put money down and signed papers before going home that day.

They had to give the Hills a longer time to get moved since they hadn't planned to move so quickly.

Now The Man and The Woman had to move out of their house. Bob Armstrong kept the dogs for awhile. While their friend J.C. was moving the dogs, they got out of the trailer and he had to chase them down the highway in the rain. The Man traded cars again. He seemed to always trade cars when they were moving. He had been trading cars and trucks so often The Woman never knew what she would be driving from one month to another. He even bought a Lincoln Continental once. The Woman hated it. She was scared she would put a scratch on it and it had too many bells and whistles to suit her. He did not keep that car very long after realizing how much a small repair would cost. So now they had a truck and a car. Eventually they moved a few things into the basement of the Hill's house and The Man and The woman moved into an apartment at the Tri State Motel. The Woman went to stay with her mother part of the time as the apartment was very claustrophobic.

Very soon after they moved in, The Woman was expecting company. Kathy had come because Jim's friend Robin and her children were visiting from Alaska. He wanted to bring them so his sister and niece could meet them.

The Woman was just starting to fix lunch when the drain under the sink began to leak. Naturally, The Man was at work. She and Kathy went to a hardware store to get a new pipe. The woman there was very helpful and they were soon busy fixing the drain. After working for an hour Kathy said she believed this was the wrong pipe. So they went back. Sure enough, the sales lady said there was another type and that's why it didn't fit. It took Kathy a short time to get the drain pipe fixed.

It looked as if they were going to have a lot of visitors at this place also. It was much different than living on the mountain or by the river so she hoped her children would be able to come and enjoy the lake.

Bobbie Jean's Baby Dress
August 1984 - Pomme de Terre

Brian and Sharon came to visit. They were going to move to Alaska soon. Also they brought their new baby girl to show The Woman. Now they had two cute little girls. The Man's sister and brother-in-law, Charlye and Johnny were there also. The Woman had bought a dress for the baby and a toy for Tonya.

While everyone was oohing and ahhing over the baby, Tonya had disappeared into the other room.

Then she waltzed in wearing Bobbie's baby dress. How she got her two year old self stuffed into that dress was a mystery. The Woman told Sharon they would probably have to cut it off of her. But Brian, being mechanically inclined, was able to get her loose from the dress and get her own clothes back on. Then they had to get back to Parkville and prepare for their trip to Alaska.

Roy Williams Died
1989 - Pomme De Terre

Roy Williams died April, 28, 1989 in Clinton, Missouri Marvin Johnson called.

Del Nabors called later to see if The Man was going to the funeral. He said he was not going.

The Man and The Woman had been to the Williams' Ranch near Leeton, Missouri before Roy went to the Medical prison in Springfield.

Snowstorm
Pomme de Terre

It was the month of March. During the night an unexpected snowstorm had begun. The Man, after he looked out the window, frantically ate a bite of breakfast and began packing extra clothes to take to work. He was working in Springfield, Missouri at a Yellow freight terminal as a class B mechanic. It was still snowing and the wind was blowing the snow around in near blizzard conditions. The Woman didn't know how he would ever make the fifty mile drive to work. The snow was already ten inches deep and there wouldn't be a snow plow through that area for days and maybe not then.

When The Man got as far as the dam on the highway that connected to Highway 65, he couldn't see whether anyone was coming from the other direction. He just had to take a chance and drive on.

Thirty minutes after he left The Woman got a phone

call. The male voice asked if her husband was coming to work. She told him The Man had left long ago. The caller said, "It's a damn good thing." That was the only time any one had ever called about The Man using that tone of voice. The Woman figured the freak snow storm was causing everyone problems. The Man had gotten within a half of a mile from work before he had to get out and walk. He stayed in Springfield the rest of the week.

The Woman's little friend, Darla, was overjoyed at the abundance of snow. Darla was a precocious seven year old who had a large imagination. The Woman often let her come to visit to play cards, or go for walks. But today they would be building things out of snow. First, they built several truck drivers, The Woman never knew what Darla was going to come up with. She thought it was odd she wanted to build truck driver snowmen. They made two children and a penguin. After that, they built a sofa and some chairs to make a living room. They fixed some hot chocolate and sat in their snow room and looked at the iced over lake. Then it was time for Darla to go home.

Margaret
Pomme de Terre

The Man told The Woman that Bill, a fellow he had met at the VFW, had a heart attack. He said Bill's wife, Margaret couldn't drive. He asked The Woman if she would take Margaret to the Bolivar hospital so she could visit him.

The Woman called Margaret who told her she was expecting one of her husband's friends to come by to take her. The Woman left her phone number and told her to call if she needed a ride. Margaret called thirty minutes later and said this fellow hadn't come yet so she would appreciate a ride to the hospital.

As time went by, they became good friends. Since Bill couldn't drive for quite awhile after he came home, The Woman and Margaret did their shopping together. Margaret liked shopping with another woman as Bill used to sit in the car while she shopped for groceries or at Walmart. She enjoyed taking her time looking at everything without having the feeling she needed to hurry. The Woman also introduced her to garage sales as she had never been to one. Margaret was a great gardener. She loved growing her own vegetables and picking gooseberries. When they got better acquainted she told The Woman about her work in Washington D.C. She had been a high ranking secretary in The Department of Agriculture where she worked for thirty years.

After Bill died The Woman would drive Margaret's car to take her shopping and to do her errands. Margaret always bought lunch and paid her although The Woman did not expect to be paid. Eventually, Margaret approached the subject of driving. She thought she could learn to drive. The Woman took her to a little park where there was almost no traffic in the off season at the lake. Margaret handled the car very well so The Woman told her she should get someone to teach her. The Woman knew that Margaret would have dozens of questions of why this and why that. She would need someone who would teach her the right way to drive. She was lucky to find the man who taught driving at the high school and he was willing to teach her. It was a wonderful day when she passed her driver's tests and could drive to the nearest town. She was an independent woman and it gave her great satisfaction to be able to drive her car.

They still visited and The Woman still drove when they went to Bolivar. Every Thanksgiving The Woman cooked the dinner for any of her children who could come. They always invited Margaret. She became a part of the family. The Man was always the one who would go get Margaret and bring her to the dinner.

When she became too ill to attend, The Woman and her children packed up a dinner and took it to her.

One day when The Woman went to get Margaret for a doctor appointment, her door was locked and she didn't come to the door. She had given a key to her several months ago. The Woman went in to find Margaret sitting on the bed. She helped her get dressed and took her to her doctor. He wanted to send her by ambulance right away to the hospital. But she said she had business at the bank she had to take care of before she left. The doctor knew it was useless to argue with her. The Woman helped her to the nearby bank. They said she would have to go in a different door to get to her safe deposit box. The Woman helped Margaret, who was in so much pain she could hardly walk, out the front door and up some steps to another door. Once in, Margaret said she had left her key at the house. She told The Woman where it was so she could go back and get it. She conducted her business there and they went back to the doctor's office. He immediately called the ambulance and sent her to the hospital. The Woman drove Margaret's car to her house and got in her truck and went home. This had been an exhausting day.

The Woman went to visit Margaret and she told her she had broken her tailbone so she didn't know where she would go from there. They had given her medication for pain and she was very groggy. But she was able to ask The Woman if she would go get all the perishable food out of her refrigerator and check the house.

Two days later The Woman received a phone call from Margaret. In spite of the heavy medication she was lucid to the point that she could dial ten numbers on the long distance phone card she had with her. Then dial the seven numbers to get The Woman on the phone. She gave The Woman the name and phone number of a rehabilitation facility where the hospital was sending her in Shawnee, Kansas. She hung up then as she was unable to talk any longer. The Woman thought since her daughters, Linda and Terisa both lived in the area of the facility, perhaps they could visit Margaret.

Three days later The Woman received a call from the Hickory County sheriff who was trying to find out where Margaret was. He said her neighbor had been gone and when she got back she couldn't get Margaret on the phone and she didn't come to the door. The sheriff had called her niece in California and she did not know where Margaret was. The Woman told him the name of the facility and the phone number. He thought it was suspicious that The Woman knew where she was and no one else did. The next day The Woman received a phone call from the receptionist at her doctor's office. She also wanted to know where Margaret was. When The Woman told her she heard the receptionist tell the doctor.

He said, "Give me that phone." Then to The Woman,

"Where is she? How come you know where she is? Nobody informed me that she was being moved."

The Woman who had never liked Margaret's doctor in the first place, told him very calmly that Margaret had called and told her where the hospital was sending her and she supposed that they had informed him. He gave the phone back to the receptionist and told her to write down the phone number and address of the rehabilitation facility.

Terisa took her two children to see Margaret often for the duration of her stay. The two kids were quite entertaining and sang songs. Linda also visited her and took little items she thought she would enjoy.

After Margaret went home she hired a young couple to help her and drive her to doctor appointments and such things. The Woman visited when she could, but her arthritis prevented her from being of any further help.

O.T.
Pomme de Terre

The Woman was putting the last of the breakfast dishes into the dishwasher when she heard the rear doorbell ring. When she opened the door, a short slightly built man wearing boots, jeans, and a cowboy hat quickly stepped in and set a large box of peaches on the counter. Before she could say anything he explained on his way out that he had been down south and bought a truckload of peaches. The Woman managed to ask him how much they cost. "You don't owe me anything" he replied as he stepped out the door, "Tell The Man I'll take it out of his hide," he joked.

O.T. was a man The Woman had met when she and The Man were returning from a popular orchard near Collins, Missouri. They had traveled down a series of narrow roads, dusty, with grass growing between the tire tracks. They came upon a car that was moving less than sixty miles per hour. The Man passed it with no room to spare. The Woman listened for the screeching of metal that never came. She had never heard of anyone passing on a country lane.

Soon they came to an old house that had been embellished with a front porch made of rough logs. Outside were several shirtless men wearing straw hats or caps working in the garden. Another tall thin man in a pair of overalls which were a few sizes too large was tinkering with the engine in an old rusty pickup truck. The Man went to the door while The Woman sat outside. The door opened and he went in. Soon he opened the door and waved for The Woman to come in. In the kitchen area she noticed a man wearing faded jeans chopping vegetables. O.T. was seated at the table. He spoke to her and asked how she was. He talked about the latest party the guys had and how many tomatoes they had canned. The Man and The Woman left then to drive over some more rough roads that came out on a familiar highway.

The Woman had a call later from The Man's sister who was a travel agent. She told her to let The Man know that O.T. couldn't get a ticket to Mexico because he had a prison record. Even so The Woman felt that he was the driving force that was keeping all those men fed and with a place to live. It was a kind of an unlikely commune. Or den of thieves, whichever way you want to look at it.

Is The Man at Home?
Pomme de Terre

The Woman was half in and half out of the chest type freezer as she searched for a package of chicken breasts that she knew was in there. She heard a knock on the back door. No one ever came to the front of the house. She closed the lid and went to see who was calling. There stood a fellow of medium height who looked to be about sixty-five years old. He was wearing jeans and jacket and a cap with a trucking company logo on the front. With him was a woman who was shorter, wearing jeans and a jacket, but no cap.

"Is The Man here?" He asked.

"No, he's not here right now." The Woman thought he would leave then, but it was not to be. She thought if he was a good friend of The Man, he would know that home was the last place to look for him.

"Well," the fellow said, "We will wait; maybe he will show up pretty soon."

As The Woman opened the door she thought to herself they were going to have a long wait. It could be midnight before he came in. But she refrained from saying so, because some of these drivers could be easily offended. He might think she was being rude.

She offered them a seat at the dining table so they could look out at the lake. The fellow commented on the weather and asked if the fishing was good lately. His wife had little to say after asking The Woman how she liked living here. The Woman did not have the knack of making small talk so they drifted into an uncomfortable silence. The gentleman finally asked if she had any coffee. The Woman had stopped offering coffee to visitors because they seldom accepted. However, she made some now because she certainly could use a cup herself. After the couple finished their coffee, they rose to leave.

"Well, I guess The Man must have been delayed some place. You tell him we stopped by to see him."

The Woman smiled and asked, "Who shall I say was here?"

The fellow had a hurt look on his face, "Well, you know us, we came to see you when you lived in Arkansas."

The Woman was sorry, but when they lived in Arkansas, there was company coming from Kansas City every weekend. Most of these people she had never met. The Woman and her children were living in a small five room house in the hills. The Man worked in Kansas City and came home on weekends. She never could understand why all these people wanted to come to Arkansas. There wasn't even a lake or any recreation facilities. One morning she opened the door to find Glenn asleep on the rough boards of the front porch. Why would he come to this place? He seemed to have a nice family and all the toys a man could want. When she looked out after having her coffee he was gone.

After the couple left she wrote their names down so The Man would know who came to visit.

The Bishop's Wife
Pomme de Terre

The Woman was very comfortable in her recliner as she had a book in one hand and a Mars bar in the other. Occasionally she looked up to watch the boats on Pomme de Terre Lake. She had already walked to the lake for a swim that morning. The phone rang. It was The Man calling from Joplin where he had stopped at The Rafters Lounge. He usually looked up old friends there when he was in that area. He told her he was bringing some people today for a fish supper. They were going to spend the night and go fishing the next morning. There would be a bishop and his wife, and Howard, and Marta.

After The Woman hung up the phone, she began to mull over what she just heard. She wondered where on earth her wandering man gotten acquainted with a bishop. She was never surprised at the people he invited to the house, but this was the strangest mix so far. Howard was their CPA and had been to the house often. Marta was a hostess and bartender at the lounge. It was no secret that she had been a companion to various men in that crowd. The mayor of Joplin, who was divorced and several other single men were among them. She had mentioned to The Woman recently that she had been fishing with Howard many weekends at his cabin at Grand Lake. The Woman laughed at the thought of the bishop showing up in a robe and a funny hat.

The Woman went downstairs to check the beds and make sure there were plenty of towels in the bathroom. Howard and Marta could sleep down here. The bishop and his wife could sleep in the guest room.

By the time the guests arrived The Woman had the meal under control. She had fish thawed out and ready to fry. She knew The Man would fry the fish because no East Texas Man could let a woman fry the fish, especially a woman from Missouri. She noted that the bishop was wearing khakis and a tee shirt.

After the meal The Man took everyone on a tour around the lake. They watched the news on TV. The Man then went downstairs to get the big rollaway bed which he wrestled up the steps to the living room. He could do that easily as he was a strong fellow. The Woman was speechless as she watched this scene unfold. The Man told Marta that she could sleep there. The Woman wondered if he didn't know about Marta and Howard or if he didn't think she knew. The Man then went outside to feed his dog. At the sound of the door closing, the bishop's wife raised her eye brows and said, "I guess there will be no hanky-panky in this man's house." Everyone smiled. The bishop and his wife retired to their room. Howard said goodnight and went downstairs.

The next morning The Woman and The Man cooked up a substantial breakfast. Everyone sat down to eat except the bishop's wife. The bishop went to see what was keeping her. He came back to the table, "She is taking a bath." The Woman smiled to herself at the audacity of the bishop's wife to take a leisurely bath while the rest of the group was getting ready to go fishing. *This has turned out to be a very comical weekend,* she thought. After the company left that afternoon, The Woman asked The Man, as he was taking the rollaway back downstairs, "Why did you bring that upstairs in the first place? Don't you know Marta and Howard spend weekends at his fishing cabin?" The Man looked at The Woman with a wide eyed innocent look which meant he was getting ready to lie, "No, I did not know that."

Trip to Women's Music Festival and Other fun Times With Linda's Friends and My Sister Anna Pomme de Terre Bloomington, Indiana

The Woman's daughter, Linda and her group of gay friends from Lawrence, Kansas and Kansas City banded together to go to Bloomington, Indiana to The Women's Music Festival each year for several years. Some of her friends played in a band they called Hobson's Choice. They had been friends for years and had good times. Some of these women were involved with the art show they had arranged for The Woman a few years ago.

The Woman's sister lived near Detroit, Michigan. Linda suggested one year that Anna meet her and The Woman in Bloomington since it was not a long drive. The Woman and Anna could share a motel room and have a vacation together. The Woman and Anna thought this would be a unique experience.

They found it amusing that it was taken for granted that they were a gay couple from the beginning. They attended some of the workshops and went to interesting places to eat. One evening they joined Linda at The Irish Lion for mutton stew and whiskey pie. The entertainment one night was by Sweet Honey in the Rock which they enjoyed very much. One night there was a tornado warning and four thousand women went to the basement of the theater. Everyone was calm and of course, some began to sing quietly. Anna commented that she never saw anyone drinking and she never detected the strong odor of perfume while they were there.

The Woman and her sister enjoyed their vacation there so much they went back several times.

Another time there was an interesting episode at a time when Anna was visiting Missouri. Hobson's Choice was going to play at Off The Wall Hall in Lawrence, Kansas on a Saturday night in November. The Woman, who was a clownish person, had agreed to join in on an old song, "Mama Don't Allow No Singin' Around Here." In her younger days The Woman had learned a foolish sounding mule call which involved braying, whistling, and foot stomping from a fellow from Texas who wore yellow cowboy boots. She and her sister used to go to a local club and dance with boys from a nearby air base. The Texan in the yellow boots would stop in the middle of the dance floor and perform this crazy mule call.

Linda went to Warrensburg to get The Woman and Anna to take them on the adventure to "Off The Wall" in Lawrence, Kansas. The Woman and her sister crawled into the back of an old green van with the musicians from Kansas City for the ride to Lawrence. The two sisters were having a good time out with a women's band away from their normal routines.

Off The Wall Hall didn't seem to have any heating system, so everyone kept their coats on. Beer was the only refreshment when what they needed was some hot coffee. After they got set up people began coming in. There were mostly women, but there was one man sitting at a table alone with a long black coat on. He probably thought he was going to have a warm place to hang out for awhile on a lonely Saturday night. He stayed anyway and drank a couple of beers.

The music started and the women cheered and applauded. Some of them got up and danced in the aisles. Then it was time for The Woman to join them on stage. They sang "Mama don't allow no mule calling in here" and The Woman performed her famous mule call. Everyone had a good laugh including the sad looking man in the black coat. Then it was over and Linda took her mother and aunt back to Warrensburg to her grandma's house. She was young and didn't mind driving all over the country in the middle of the night. The two sisters always had a good time with Linda and her little friends.

Plumbly Tar Music Festival
Pomme de Terre

The river that flowed through what is now Hickory County, Missouri, was named Pomme de Terre River by early French explorers. The Native Americans (before this country was called America) living in the area had shown the explorers a wild potato plant that grew along the banks of the river which was a welcome addition to their food supply.

Many years later, settlers began farming the area. Eventually a dam was built and a recreational lake named Pomme de Terre Lake came into being.

The local people had gradually fractured the fancy name of the lake into Plumbly Tar. The outsiders who moved there from nearby cities called it Spud Pond.

The Man and The Woman had lived there for two years when Toni and Phil Cox built a house next door. They were from Boston and moved back to this area to be near their son. They were caring for Phil's mother who needed full time care. Toni and The Woman became acquainted. Toni enjoyed getting out of the house for a few hours now and then to go shopping or swimming.

The Woman mentioned to Toni that her daughter, Kathy, was coming from Arkansas and would be picking up her brother Jim from the airport in Springfield. Her sister was coming from Michigan. She said she wished she knew someplace where her brother Jim could play the piano so she could record him playing and singing. He had been in Alaska and the family hadn't heard him play for a long time.

Toni exclaimed very excitedly, "Phil and I love to sing, we have a piano and an organ right here in our house. Phil has good recording equipment. We would love to have your family come and we could set up the organ and piano in the living room."

The Woman found it hard to believe that these people had all this equipment next door and that they would enjoy doing this for her. She and Toni got busy and printed up words to some of the old songs they might not remember. The Woman said she would cook a dinner to have at her house.

The Woman called her sister Betty because she and her husband, James Edward would enjoy a 'sing a long'. Betty said they would like to come and park their camper at the state park.

Jim started off the session with some old songs like "Little Brown Jug" and "She'll Be Comin' Around The Mountain". Betty would start out singing very loud but then would begin talking. She and Anna were both sopranos who were trying to out-sing each other. Sopranos always sounded off key to The Woman.

The Woman sang alto and no one cared what she was singing as they couldn't hear her over Jim the tenor and the sopranos anyway. They later referred to themselves as The Sibling Rivalry Singers. Toni and Phil were very good singers who sang a duet of "All Through the Night" when The Sibling Rivalry Singers stopped to take a breather. Kathy, while being a very intelligent girl of many talents, was discouraged from singing at an early age by The Woman. She was, however, allowed to sing "Over The River and Through The Woods" on occasion. Once when she called her sister Terisa to sing "Happy Birthday," Terisa said, "I guess you are determined to continue this to the bitter end."

In spite of the rivalry there was much laughter and talking. Jim played the organ and the piano and the entire song fest was recorded for their future enjoyment.

They all went over next door to eat a lunch of smothered steak, scalloped potatoes, green beans, slaw and apple pie.

So, The Plumbly Tar Music Festival was over. Everyone thanked the Cox's and they seemed to have enjoyed the day. The Woman had a great week of shopping at the outlet stores in Lebanon and in Bolivar with Kathy, Jim, and Anna. The Plumbly Tar Music Festival topped the week off. On Sunday everyone had to go. Linda came to take Anna to The Kansas City airport and Kathy took Jim to the one in Springfield, on her way home. Betty and James Edward packed up their camper and went home to Concordia, Missouri.

Time To Move
1991 - Pomme De Terre

After a cold snowy winter The Woman finished a project she called "Buzzard Quilts." She had made twin size quilts for each child and grandchild. This kept her busy while The Man read Westerns and watched football on TV or at the VFW Hall.

Kathy and Bill's baby finally arrived in February. Linda and The Woman made two trips to Arkansas to see the new baby.

When the weather warmed up, the little boy across the road began to be a problem. The mother worked and the teenage daughter who was supposed to be watching him was more of a problem than the boy. He had built a fire by a neighbor's house, he was into his father's tools trying to start the lawnmower, and one day The Woman saw him climb up on the roof of his house. He had been in The Man's garage at some time. The Man and the neighbor began arguing about the road and septic tanks and other things. The Man began talking about moving again. The Woman could see the writing on the wall. She had stalled him off of selling the house, but now she feared the little boy might get hurt on their property. She figured the neighbors would sue them if anything happened to him in their garage. Then drug dealers moved into the neighborhood. The neighbors The Man had been arguing with seemed to be very friendly with the new comers.

The Woman agreed to put the house up for sale. She began packing and throwing stuff out. They began going on trips looking for a new place to live.

The End

About the Author

Donna Mott is a self-taught watercolorist and writer. She has spent many years hiking in the Arkansas and Missouri Ozarks. She enjoys looking at nature. She has worked on family genealogy with her sister, Anna, and her daughter, Terisa.

Donna's previous books *Shoats, Hogs and Murder*, and *Brushy Creek Manor* were published under one cover, *Two Twiggs County Mysteries*, in 2012.

CPSIA information can be obtained at www.ICGtesting.com
Printed in the USA
LVOW11s1058121113

360964LV00004B/80/P